GREY PASTURES

BY

WILLIAM HASLAM MILLS

second edition

The Chapels Society
London
2003

THE CHAPELS SOCIETY

The Chapels Society seeks to foster public interest in and knowledge of the architectural and historical importance of all places of worship and their related structures in the UK loosely described as Nonconformist.

HON. SECRETARY
Robin Phillips
1 Newcastle Avenue
Beeston
Nottinghamshire NG9 IBT

HON. EDITOR
Joy Rowe
Haughley Grange
Stowmarket
Suffolk IPI4 3QT

First published by Chatto & Windus, London 1924
This edition, published by The Chapels Society, 2003
© The Chapels Society, 2003

ISBN 0-9545061-0-3

PRINTED FOR THE CHAPELS SOCIETY
FROM CAMERA-READY COPY BY
QUACKS THE PRINTERS
JACKSON HOUSE, 7 GRAPE LANE, PETERGATE,
YORK, YO1 7HU

CONTENTS

ILLUSTRATIONS

Fig. 1. William Haslam Mills (1874-1930)
Photo by F. W. Schmidt, Manchester

ACKNOWLEDGEMENTS

OUR first debt is to William Haslam Mills and to the *Manchester Guardian* where most of what is printed in this volume first appeared. In 1924 the author expressed his indebtedness to the proprietors of that journal for their permission to re-publish his articles and we add our thanks for permission to reprint the additional material which now comprises the last chapter. We are also indebted to Dr Douglas Farnie of the Manchester Metropolitan University for identifying this extra material. The original idea for the book was put to Mills by Thomas Southcliffe Ashton, then a senior lecturer in Economics at the University of Manchester, a younger contemporary of Haslam Mills who had grown up in that extra-ordinarily vigorous and creative community at Albion Chapel, Ashton-under-Lyne, which forms the subject matter of the book. The key to the thinly-disguised characters who appear in *Grey Pastures* is based on information provided by T. S. Ashton to his son, Anthony, who projected a second edition in 1982. Anthony Ashton wrote an extensive Introduction for this but the project was never realised. We are grateful to Mr Ashton for allowing us to use what is substantially his text as the present Introduction; to Tameside Local Studies Library for their helpfulness as we have prepared this edition; and to Professor Clyde Binfield of the University of Sheffield for sharing with us his extensive knowledge of Congregational Dissent in general and Albion Chapel in particular. The illustrations are new to this edition and we acknowledge the permission of the Science and Society Picture Library of the National Museum of Science and Industry to use the photograph from the *Illustrated London News* which appears as figure 7.

PREFACE

I WAS introduced to *Grey Pastures* by Alan Cass, a university librarian and consummate historian who carried into its *Guardian* days the virtues of the old *Manchester Guardian's* readership. He was a pacifist, a socialist, and a Methodist with a passion for cricket, an instinct for connections, and an unerring eye for stylishly accurate exposition. How he encountered *Grey Pastures* I do not know. Perhaps cricket as interpreted by Neville Cardus led him to Haslam Mills. Perhaps it was Methodism, for Alan Cass's Methodist roots were not Wesleyan but Free, indeed New Connexion, and New Connexion Methodism interlocked with Congregationalism as a formative influence for Victorian Ashton and its grey pastures.

To call *Grey Pastures* a classic (for it is no mere 'minor' classic) is to risk much. It is mannered, artful, whimsical, nostalgic, elegiac; qualities which purists now regard as defects and which instinctively arouse the distrust of Nonconformists. It is 'clever'. Its humour makes it disconcerting. It celebrates life in a minor key. But it is also accurate. It is at once sharply and subtly nuanced. It makes judgments, asks questions, encourages reflection, but it does so obliquely. It celebrates that rare art form, true journalism, and it would be hard to think of a better or more representative primary source for understanding Victorian Nonconformity.

Its accent is on Congregationalism, indeed Independency. Therefore the focus is local, the world of the *petite histoire*. But it is a world, nonetheless. Haslam Mills conveys its tone, alerts us to its far horizons, encourages us to explore its adventurous mentality. It was no longer his world, although it had formed him and he could not wholly escape it – hence his affectionately clear-eyed respect for a world which placed personal commitment at its centre but which recognised that the path to such commitment was shaped by scepticism, criticism, instinctive nonconformity, and all the frustrating limits as well as the boundless possibilities of human nature.

The Chapels Society is to be congratulated on reprinting *Grey Pastures* and Anthony Ashton has out of his family experience provided the editors with material for an Introduction which could not be bettered.

Clyde Binfield

INTRODUCTION

THIS is a book of humour: witty, gently ironic, mostly affectionate, beautifully written by a craftsman skilled with words. It is also a sensitive and penetrating commentary on life, in one part of the country at least, towards the end of the nineteenth century.

The book as published in 1924 consisted of eighteen sketches reconstructed from articles which first appeared in the *Manchester Guardian* between 1912 and 1919. Mills himself added chapter XVIII as new material and the present edition also includes as chapter XIX a further *Manchester Guardian* essay omitted from the original. The subject matter is mainly the social life surrounding a Congregational chapel in a middle-sized Lancashire manufacturing town in the later Gladstonian era – grey pastures indeed! The author was writing about the world of his childhood, seen first with the sharp senses of a child and then savoured in the mind of a highly intelligent and sensitive adult. As he writes, it is clear that he has grown out of that world, seeing its absurdities and hypocrisies just as clearly as he sees the value of its aspirations and achievements. But through all the sketches runs a nostalgic affection for a world that has gone, a world in which a certain group of people imbued with strong conviction, great confidence, quite astonishing energy and, one could add, considerable wealth, formed a living community that embraced all sides of life – religious, intellectual, artistic, social and, not least, political.

This is no work of fiction. Mills draws a thin veil over the people and places he writes about by giving them fictitious names, but he makes no other effort to disguise them, and it must have been part of the fun for many of his readers when the sketches first appeared to identify the characters. *Grey Pastures* is about a real chapel in a real town, at a real period of time. Anthony Ashton recalls:

> My first meeting with this book was when I was a boy. It was on the bookshelf in the sitting-room, and was distinguished by being the only book that must never be taken out of the house, lest it be lost or damaged. The reason for this became clear later. The book was about my parents' own childhood and growing up, as it was about the author's. They knew it all: they had been to the same chapel, the same Sunday school, the same day school, had lived in the same closely-knit community and taken part in the same solemnities and festivities; they recognised the people and places, the events and the attitudes, the sights

and sounds and scents. Above all they enjoyed – somewhere between laughter and tears – the delightful humour with which the book is written.

The town, which Mills calls Ashton-on-the-Hill, is Ashton-under-Lyne, a few miles east of Manchester. The chapel, which he calls Wycliffe, was Albion Congregational Chapel, and the period is, broadly, the 1880s. The people in the sketches are all drawn faithfully from life. For example, Mr. Harkness was the Rev. John Hutchison, minister of Albion for thirty-two years; Henry Stonor was Hugh Mason, undoubtedly the most important man in Ashton, mill-owner and philanthropist, mayor and MP. And there are many others. At the end of this Introduction there is a list of the main characters in the sketches with their real names and some notes about them.

Dissent in Ashton

The administrative machinery and financial system of the Church of England was quite unable to cope with the spreading influence of the evangelical revival and expansion of population that accompanied industrialisation in the eighteenth century, Nor, so far as Ashton was concerned, did it appear to be trying very hard. In 1816, the then lord of the manor, the fifth Earl of Stamford and Warrington, presented the living of St Michael's parish church to his grandson, who later also became vicar of Chilton, a pleasant village in Buckinghamshire, where he lived until 1870, leaving his less attractive northern parish to two over-worked curates. True, another church (St Peter's) was built in Ashton in 1824, but it was starved of funds, most of which continued to go to St Michael's. Many who sought a more lively expression of their faith found it beyond the confines of Church of England. Perhaps also the bleak countryside with its harsh climate was responsible for a people long noted for their stubborn independence, determined to bow down to no bishop or hereditary landlord. This was a new society in which self-help and independence were the watchwords of a newly self-made and upwardly mobile elite.

By the mid-nineteenth century there had developed an astonishing variety of religious denominations: several different kinds of Methodists – Wesleyans, Primitives, New Connexion and United Free Churches; there were also Baptists and Anabaptists, Swedenborgians and Christian Israelites, Stephensites and Barkerites and others. There were of course, some members of the Church of England, and there were a few Roman

Catholics (mostly Irish immigrants) but above all, there were the Independents. The latter were particularly well-suited to the people of Ashton as their very name implies. They wanted to run things themselves, and by the mid-nineteenth century the Independents, now known as Congregationalists, had emerged as the strongest religious and social force in Ashton.

It was against this background that the congregation of Albion chapel was formed, grew and flourished. The story of the chapel begins about 1815 when a group of seceders from Providence Chapel, in nearby Dukinfield, started meeting in an ex-Methodist chapel in Ashton. The following year they opened what was known as 'The Refuge' chapel and in 1818 Jonathan Sutcliffe was invited to become the first minister. He came of a family of farmers at Rawtenstall on the edge of the Pennines. Beginning as a clergyman in the Church of England, he turned Independent because, it was said, he wanted more scope for preaching. He was highly successful and the congregation grew rapidly, so that in 1827 the chapel had to be enlarged. Then, in 1835, a new and larger chapel was built alongside in Albion Street. This was the chapel (illustrated on the cover) in which the young Mills grew up and later wrote about so vividly. When Jonathan Sutcliffe retired, his place was taken by Dr Guinness Rogers who became somewhat of a celebrity in the country: he was appointed Chairman of the Congregational Union and even gained the friendship of Mr Gladstone himself. He left Albion after fourteen years to take charge of the church at Grafton Square, Clapham, and Mills mentions him (by his real name) in the context of a reported visit to London (p. 28). He was succeeded by John Hutchison, the Mr Harkness of *Grey Pastures*, who was minister for thirty-two years (see fig. 4).

The Families

Clyde Binfield has emphasised the importance in the Congregational movement of certain large and influential families. The main influence at Albion was exerted by three: the Sutcliffes, Buckleys and Masons.

Jonathan Sutcliffe, the first Minister of Albion, has already been mentioned. He married Susan Collier Buckley, daughter of Nathaniel Buckley of Crows-i'-th'-Wood, and this marriage was to prove of great importance to Albion. Jonathan was poor, and there is a harrowing account handed down in the family of how Susan only buttered alternate pieces of bread that went on the tea-table, and saw that he got the buttered ones, while his thoughts were doubtless occupied with his sermons. His father-in-law, Nathaniel, was a cotton spinner who had a small mill worked by water, but refused to instal a steam engine because 'the devil was in it'. However, his sons, James and Abel, were more enterprising and did well out of cotton in Ashton. The Buckleys became wealthy, and Abel's son (of the same name) gave considerable sums of money to Albion, underwriting the school building and providing nearly half the funds needed for the new church that was built in 1890-5. It was this marriage of religion and wealth that gave so much force to Albion's activities.

Not surprisingly, one of Jonathan's sons, Nathaniel Buckley Sutcliffe, combined these two strands and had a big influence on Albion. He was a master cotton spinner. He was also a well-educated and humane man who kept his workers employed through the Cotton Famine of the 1860s (when the American Civil War stopped the export of cotton). He married Martha Anne, daughter of William Sunderland who was headmaster of the Stamford Academy, a school for middle-class boys in Ashton. He saw to it that his children had an excellent schooling: one of his daughters, Susan, was sent to Edinburgh to 'finish' her education, and his son, William, was sent to France to learn about cotton spinning there. Two other daughters, Margaret and Florence, became teachers and travelled widely on the continent. Nathaniel Buckley Sutcliffe was a deacon of Albion for more than fifty years, and a superintendent at the Sunday School. There is a fitting tribute to him in a tablet in the 'new' Albion church. The Sutcliffes were the 'Surridges' referred to by Mills. They were, he says, 'distraught with new-fangled ideas'. One of the Miss Surridges 'went to Germany and returned pronouncing Lancashire names like Mendelssohn and Mozart as they are pronounced in Prague'.

Hugh Mason

The Buckleys and Sutcliffes had a great influence upon Albion, but when Mills was a boy there is no doubt that it was Hugh Mason (the 'Henry Stonor' of Mills's sketches) who was the most important man in Ashton, and who dominated the Albion congregation (in so far as anyone *could* dominate such people). He appears in several places in *Grey Pastures*, and also has a whole chapter to himself (see fig. 5). He was born in 1817. His father, Thomas, started work in a cotton mill at the age of eight, went to night school, saved money and started up in business in a small way. He prospered and built several cotton mills; diversified into coal, iron and railways, and became rich: the Masons were one of the leading families in Ashton. Hugh was the third son. He started work in a mill at ten, but was later sent to the Stamford Academy run by Mr Sunderland.

When Hugh was forty-five he took control of his father's mills. Like his father, he wished to be a good employer: his mills were, by the standards of the day, well-built and spacious; there were hot baths and a swimming pool, a gymnasium and a sports ground. In 1871 he became the first local employer to grant his workers Saturday afternoon off. He insisted that they sent their children to Sunday School, abstained from alcohol, did not gamble or go to the theatre. Young men had to give up tobacco ('and so for a time, and in public, they did', commented Mills). If a man did not turn up for work, his wife was sent for to explain why. He would have no trade unionists. He became in turn Mayor of Ashton, President of the Manchester Chamber of Commerce, and finally in 1880 Member of Parliament for Ashton. He lived in some style at Groby Hall (called 'Granite Hall' by Mills) with a carriage, coachman and footmen, and had a town house in Onslow Square in London. He began as a Methodist like his father but left them about 1846 when he married Sarah Buckley and joined the congregation at Albion, where he remained until his death in 1886. When he died, most people in Ashton stopped work for the day and many lined the way to the cemetery. They put up a statue to him. When it was unveiled the streets were decorated, the bands marched and the town was said to be awash with beer - Mason would have turned in his grave!

Mills did not like him. Indeed, he is the only character in the book about whom he writes anything disobliging. It was part of the process of Mills's growing up, and he was writing at a time when the reaction against Victorian values was at its strongest. Mason's magnanimity and welfare paternalism were no doubt sincere but could seem patronising, as when at the Albion Christmas dinner during the Cotton Famine in 1862, he eloquently congratulated 'that noble, manly, self-reliant, self-sacrificing, peaceful, intelligent, loyal spirit of the working classes of Lancashire'.

The Schools

The Sunday School has already been briefly mentioned. This played an important part in the life of Albion. When Mills was a boy, the attendance was more than a thousand scholars in the morning, and fifteen hundred in the afternoon. The school was taken very seriously, as being the foundation of the congregation, and the teachers, or 'superintendents' as they were called, were mainly drawn from the congregation itself: most of the worthies who appear in Mills's sketches were at one time or another superintendents of the Sunday school, some for many years: for example, James Ogden Taylor, Nathaniel Buckley Sutcliffe, Abraham Park, Daniel Fowler Howorth, Jonas Knight, and the great Hugh Mason himself. Many others, while not superintendents, were very active in support of the school in other ways, such as George Harrison and Miss Ripley. Altogether about two hundred teachers were needed, and most of them had in their time been scholars at the school. It was a great 'do-it-yourself' exercise that aimed to combine religious and secular instruction of a high quality. The school was very successful, and led to the opening of a day school in 1869, many years ahead of its time in the quality of scientific and technical education provided. Abraham Park became headmaster. As it developed, the school took children right through from the start up to university entrance.

It is important to realise the scale of all this educational activity. The new school building, 'pseudo-Italian in style', that was opened in 1862 was very large (see fig. 6). The opening service in that year was attended by two thousand people in what was justifiably, if somewhat modestly, known as 'the large room' (see fig. 7). At the time, it was claimed that this was the largest denominational school in England.

The Church

The congregation continued to grow with the town, and so outgrew the Albion Street chapel. New premises were needed, and nothing less than a full-sized church in the gothic style would do, with everything of the very best. The architect was John Brooke of Manchester. The church was to seat a thousand, the spire was two-hundred and twenty feet high, the stained-glass windows were designed by Burne-Jones and executed by William Morris, and the organ was the most advanced - and expensive - in the country (some said, in Europe). And so it was built, on high ground, to the east of the town-centre, on the site previously occupied by Mr. Sunderland's Stamford Academy. It cost about £50,000, an enormous sum for those days. The 'Independents' had come a long way from the austere times of the old 'Refuge' chapel. Indeed, some of the congregation had doubts about the gothic style and stained-glass windows. Were they not supposed to be against such things?

It was an astonishing achievement, and clearly a source of great satisfaction to congregation and elders alike. Undoubtedly some of the satisfaction came from remembering their humble beginnings and early difficulties; and in knowing that the new church was bigger, taller, and had a larger congregation than the parish church, which it now (in two senses) could look down upon. Hugh Mason is quoted as having said, 'even in religious matters we are none the worse for a little wholesome and salutary competition'. Mills cannot have heard

Fig. 2. The new Albion Church, opened 1895

of that remark, for if he had he would surely have used it with devastating effect.

The Activities

There was the chapel, and later, the church. There was the Sunday school, and later the day school. But this was by no means the whole of it. Albion was the centre of an extraordinarily vigorous range of spiritual and social activities: a Working Men's Class, a Mothers' Class, a Young Women's Christian Aid Society, a Band of Hope, a Library, a Literary Society, a Christian Usefulness Society, a Tract Society, a Choir and a Dorcas Society which made clothes for the poor. A full-time paid 'town missionary' made over 3,000 visits a year to the poorer houses of the town. Albion might also be described as the unofficial headquarters of the Ashton Liberal Party. The Literary Society had an astonishing range. In one session, for example, there were thirty lectures, with subjects ranging from 'Congregational Independency characteristic of the Apostolic churches' to the history of signboards. The minister, Mr. Hutchison, gave three lectures, on the life of Sir Walter Scott, the story of Queen Elizabeth's reign as told by Shakespeare, and 'Furnished Lodgings, with Illustrations'. Mills's father, James, lectured on Mendelssohn in relation to the Psalmody, Abraham Park on the Revolution of 1688, and even Dr. Hamilton made one of his rare appearances and lectured on 'Popular Physiology'. Daniel Fowler Howorth lectured on 'Folk's Speech of Lancashire', and later became responsible for a monthly study of English literature. Here again we find the Albion 'do-it-yourself' system hard at work: nearly every lecturer was a member of the Society, and therefore of the ·congregation.

Hugh Mason, for all his puritanical prejudices, was a widely read man. The intellectual interests of the Sutcliffes have already been mentioned and how they were 'distraught with new-fangled ideas'. Nathaniel Buckley Sutcliffe used surreptitiously to pass copies of such journals as the *Nineteenth Century* over the pew-back at Sunday morning service to his nephew. This practice of passing round the latest weighty periodicals at chapel is also associated by Mills with Charles Timothy Bradbury (Mills's Mr Darlington), and the 'fearful outbreak of Egyptology' in the Bradbury family is a good example of the wide-ranging interests of these people, and also an example of the family links in the Congregational world. The Bradburys were friends of Elkanah Armitage (a Congregational minister and theologian) and his wife, Ella Sophia (a pioneer student at Newnham College). The Armitages were deeply interested in Egyptology, and Elkanah's sister, Marion, married Jesse Haworth, who provided some of the funds for Flinders Petrie's earlier expeditions. In 1880 (when Mills was six) the Armitages and Haworth went to Egypt, and after they came back Elkanah and Ella gave many lectures about it. Jesse Haworth endowed the Egyptology collection of the Manchester Museum. He also subscribed to the building of the new Albion church. The Armitages and Haworths were influential members of the Congregational church at Bowdon, a well-to-do outer suburb of Manchester, and there was clearly close contact – and some rivalry – between Albion and Bowdon Downs. The Mills family was linked by marriage to the Armitages and 'Uncle William, whose formidable code of morals was unimpaired even by the lassitudes and laxities of living in Bowdon', was actually John Mills, James Mills's brother, married to Isabel Petrie.

Money

All this great and varied activity needed money and, particularly because of the building operation, very large amounts of money. We forget just how much money could be made by an energetic industrialist, given an expanding market in days before heavy taxation and control by the state. They made it, and they gave to Albion. They gave for a variety of reasons: because it was the highest thing they knew; because they wanted to do good; because they wanted to be seen to be doing good; because others gave; because they gained prestige and influence by doing so. Whatever their motives and however mixed, they gave.

Nothing was stinted. The minister was paid £500 a year, more than the Town Clerk received. This was a far cry from Susan Sutcliffe's alternately buttered slices of bread! When the new school was built at a total cost of £11,000, a sum of £1,300 was collected at the opening in 1862 and a further £4,000 or more soon afterwards even though this was during the depressed days of the Cotton Famine. Because of the Famine, the subscription lists were closed until the trade recovered, and the debt was carried until 1867, when it was cleared by means of a bazaar. Though it was before his time, Mills would have heard the debt referred to.

> Though considerable in amount and not slightly overdue, the debt was wholly free from that moral taint which attaches to the unpaid bills of individuals. Perhaps the difference was faintly indicated in the words in which they referred to its extinction - it was not so much to be 'paid' as to be 'wiped out'.

And wiped out it well and truly was. At the opening ceremony of the bazaar, Hugh Mason, who was then Treasurer, said that if they could raise £4,000 he would guarantee the rest would be found by private subscription, and the mill owner, Abel Buckley, for his part, said that if they could raise £3,800 he would make up the difference to £4,000. In the event, they raised £4,013.2s.3d. The culmination of it all, the building of the new Albion church, cost as we have seen £50,000, yet when it opened in 1895 it was already free from debt – owing particularly to the munificence of Abel Buckley who gave no less than £23,000.

Bazaars

Apart from the private contributions of individuals, bazaars were an important source of funds. Albion was famous for its bazaars, and there was doubtless a great desire to make each more impressive than the last. Mills writes, 'The bazaar during the long period of its approach ceased to figure in talk as the Bazaar, and was known colloquially and without the need of further particularization as "the great effort".' The official report of the bazaar of 1867 refers to it as 'the large effort to clear the debt from the Schools'. It should be explained that in his sketch, 'The Big Bazaar', Mills was combining what was always known as 'the Grand Bazaar' of 1867 which was held seven years before he was born, with the semi-Jubilee of Albion Schools, held in 1887 when he was thirteen, and it is the details of the latter that he is describing in *Grey Pastures*.

On this latter occasion, according to the official record, 'a strong committee was appointed'. It was chaired by Abraham Park, 'the active and energising spirit ... to whom the great success which has attended this celebration is largely due'. On the committee were also Nathaniel Buckley Sutcliffe and, of course, James Ogden Taylor, without whom no function of any importance at Albion could be organised.

The celebrations lasted for a week, beginning with a religious service and ending with a 'conversazione'. The official account of the proceedings runs as follows:

> there were exhibited an interesting and valuable collection of pictures, missionary articles, microscopes, books, and a varied assortment of objects of value and attraction. Vocal and instrumental selections were given at intervals – the larger room was decorated in the most handsome manner ... it presented the appearance of a gigantic private drawing room, toned by a warmth of comfort which enhanced the art of the decoration.

The 'tableaux vivants', so delightfully described by Mills, were an important attraction, the result, he says, of 'a bold and innovating spirit which disclosed itself in the entertainments' (see fig. 3). Even the official record is rather tongue-in-cheek about them:

> One of the most marked and attractive features in the evening entertain-

ments provided for the visitors during Thursday, Friday and Saturday, is that known under the designation of tableaux vivants - a new feature entirely in amusements in Ashton-under-Lyne. Divested of the French designation they may be described as living pictures, brought out in fuller realistic grouping in details by coloured lights.

Envoi

It could not last for ever. The Albion congregation continued to grow until the early years of the twentieth century, but before then its main thrust was over and the long Victorian afternoon was coming to an end. New forces were at work. Church-going was in decline, Sunday schools were no longer regarded as so important. The day schools were swept into the state system. The First World War brought great social and political changes. Trade unions increased in power, and the cotton industry decayed. Many people came to look elsewhere for their aspirations and satisfaction, and for their social life.

The old 'Refuge' chapel where Jonathan Sutcliffe used to preach and which became the headquarters of the Ashton PSA (Pleasant Sunday Afternoon), made way in the 1990s for a doctors' surgery with only a plaque to mark the site. The Albion chapel referred to in *Grey Pastures* was pulled down in 1964. The large school building has survived, but is used as a warehouse. However, the 'new' church stands elegantly on its green mound, obviously well-cared for. The Burne-Jones windows gleam as richly as they did when William Morris made them, portraying figures representing various Christian virtues and saints emblematic of them. The fine organ which Mills's father played is in excellent condition. On the walls tablets commemorate Hugh Mason, Nathaniel Buckley and Nathaniel Buckley Sutcliffe. In its own way, so too does Mills's delightfully evocative *Grey Pastures*.

The Author

William Haslam Mills was born in 1874 in Ashton. His father, James Mills, was the music critic on the *Manchester Examiner*, and for many years the organist at Albion. Haslam Mills, as he liked to be called, was educated at Manchester Grammar School and joined the staff of the *Manchester Guardian* at the age of twenty-one. He spent a few years in the press gallery of the House of Commons, but then left to work for a while on *The Times*. He returned to the *Manchester Guardian* in 1904 where he remained until 1919. For the last five years of his time with the *Guardian*, he was Chief Reporter. Those who worked on the *Manchester Guardian* in those days under the vigilant leadership of C. P. Scott, were an elite, a privileged few meeting standards far beyond the reach of ordinary journalists.

Indeed, they did not call themselves 'journalists' but 'writers'. And that is what they were, though in the special sense of writers who wrote for the *Manchester Guardian*.

In 1919 Mills became Director of Public Information at the Ministry of Health but left in 1920 to work as a freelance writer. In 1921 he wrote the centenary history of the *Manchester Guardian*. He finally turned his hand to writing advertising copy, and teaching others how to do so. He died in 1930 at the age of 56. *Grey Pastures* is his best – and best-known – book.

What kind of man was he? His portrait conveys a strong impression of drama: and he was indeed very much a man of the theatre, going often and writing many notices of plays (see fig. 1). There is more than a hint of Mills's love of the theatre in two of his sketches 'On having seen Irving' and 'The First Violin'. Neville Cardus provides a detailed description in his *Autobiography*:

> He was tall and elegant and thin; grey hair was brushed straight back from his fine but not too high forehead; his eyes were deep-set, and when he spoke sitting down, his chin would tend to sink to his shirt-front, and then his eyes gleamed at you upwards. They were sensitive eyes which seemed to look not only at whoever was with him, but inward at himself; and I always felt they were observant less of one's appearance and movements than of one's choice of words. His face was deathly white and his mouth was keen, but not hard, and two deep lines were graven down each cheek. He was almost spectacularly handsome and he wore his clothes perfectly, with the right looseness. He favoured a soft striped collar and a bow; somehow he so arranged his neckwear that it suggested a cravat. His fingers were long and feminine ... There was no stiffness, not an angle, about him; he was all curves. None the less he never gave a hint of a casual attitude or a low temperature; he relaxed as though with a feline reserve power of suppleness and springiness.

Mills was above all a stylist, in writing as well as in dress and conversation. Howard Spring, who was trained at the *Manchester Guardian* by Mills, recalled how 'Everything about him was neat'. The core of his writing is the clear, direct prose demanded by the *Manchester Guardian* in C. P. Scott's day. But he turned this to his own purpose, with a deft embroidery that made a vehicle for his own particular kind of ironic humour and keen perception of people, places and events. After all, he was a reporter: the best the *Manchester Guardian* had, and that was inevitably very good indeed. In *Grey Pastures* he brought this reporting skill to a high level of artistry, describing the details of his childhood with a vivid and evocative precision. In Spring's informed opinion, the book 'reproduces the atmosphere of provincial Liberalism and Nonconformity with a tender and whimsical appreciation that I have not known equalled'. Mills had the capacity to invest events trivial in themselves with significance. Often, the reader realises only afterwards that he has made a serious point, he does it so lightly and unobtrusively. He was, recalled Spring, 'a brilliant journalist; a character of great originality'.

Further Reading

Binfield, J. C. G., 'In Search of Mrs "A": a transpennine quest', *United Reformed Church History Society Transactions* 3, pp. 234-51.

Binfield, J. C. G., 'The Dynamic of Grandeur. Albion Church, Ashton-under-Lyne', *Transactions of the Lancashire and Cheshire Antiquarian Society* 85 (1988), pp. 173-92.

Cardus, N., *Autobiography* (London 1947, reprinted 1975), pp. 94-95.

Glover, W., *A History of Ashton-under-Lyne and the Surrounding District* (Ashton-under-Lyne, 1884), pp. 248-73.

Holland, J., 'Hugh Mason' in Harrop, S. A. and Rose, E. A., eds, *Victorian Ashton* (Ashton-under-Lyne, 1974), pp. 7-15.

Rose, E. A., 'Ashton Churches and Chapels' in Harrop and Rose, pp. 60-75.

Spring, H., *In the Meantime* (London, 1942, reprinted 1943), pp. 91-95.

CHARACTERS

Miss Cheeseman:

> Almost certainly Emma Hilton (rhymes with Stilton!) who appears in the records as having won a prize for Scripture History in 1873. The famous 'Tableaux Vivants' took place fourteen years later.

Mr Darlington:

> Charles Timothy Bradbury (1827-1907). Cotton spinner (who always stood for prayers!). Member of a wealthy and influential Congregational family. Friend of the Armitages and Haworths, and thus 'into' Egyptology. He was involved in the setting up of the Albion day schools.

Mr Dillworth:

> Daniel Fowler Howorth (1842-1919). A superintendent at the Sunday School for eleven years. Active in the literary society, and joint secretary of the Grand Bazaar of 1867.

John Ogden Green:

> James Ogden Taylor (1834-1897). Haslam Mills's uncle. A tailor and haberdasher. The souvenir published in 1912 on the occasion of the Jubilee of Albion Schools says 'Outside of his business, the Sunday Schools were all in all to him'. He became a superintendent in 1862 and later secretary of the school committee, and was involved in almost everything to do with organisation at Albion.

Mr Harkness:

> Rev. John Hutchison (1824-1899). The third Minister of Albion Chapel (and later Minister of the Church). Educated at Glasgow Theological Hall. He came to Albion in 1865, and remained as Minister for 32 years, retiring in 1898. He died the next year. 'His preaching was full of evangelical power, appealing to the intellect as well as the emotion of his hearers.'

John Hills:

> James Mills (1828-1897), Haslam Mills's father. He was music critic of the *Manchester Examiner*, and for thirty years the organist at Albion.

Dr Macfarlane:

> Dr Alexander Hamilton. A rare attender! Gave a lecture to the Literary Society in 1873 on 'Popular Physiology'. Attended Mrs. Clarke at the 'Big Bazaar' in 1887. He graduated in 1865 and died in Edinburgh, 1926.

Aunt Margaret:

> Mrs. John Mills, née Petrie. Haslam Mills's aunt, who lived at Bowdon. Her husband (James Mills's brother) was a banker with the Lancashire and Yorkshire bank. She wrote the *Threads from the Life of John Mills* (1899)

Aunt Mary:

> Mrs. Samuel Mills, another of Haslam Mills's aunts. Member of Ashton Methodist New Connexion Chapel, Stamford Street.

Mrs Scrape:

> Mrs. Clarke. Wife of the Chapel-keeper.

Fred Space:

> Jim Park. Either son or brother of Abraham Park (see below). He was an accountants' clerk and sang solo tenor in the choir. Clearly a bit of a wag. Married Margaret, Mills's sister.

Jacob Space:

> Abraham Park (1837-1917). Headmaster of the day schools from 1869, and a superintendent of the Sunday schools from 1874 to 1892. Educated at Glasgow University. Chairman of the Higher Education Committee 'for a very large district under the Lancashire County Council'. Born in Rutherglen. Founder of Ashton PSA.

Henry Stonor:

> Hugh Mason (1817-1886). Ashton's leading citizen, being in turn its Mayor and Member of Parliament. Mill-owner, puritan and philanthropist. Educated at Mr. Sunderland's Stamford Academy in Ashton. At one time President of the Manchester Chamber of Commerce. Deacon of Albion.

The Surridges:

> The Sutcliffes. Jonathan Sutcliffe was the first Minister of Albion. His son Nathaniel Buckley Sutcliffe was a master cotton-spinner who, along with his brother Edward and brother-in-law Walker Sunderland, owned three factories. Nathaniel Buckley Sutcliffe (1828-1908) was a deacon of the chapel and church for fifty years, and a superintendent at the Sunday School for six. His son William and daughters Susan, Margaret and Florence, were well-educated and travelled widely on the continent.

Mr Tame:

> Mr Wild, the milkman.

Mr. Walmsley:

> George Harrison (1821-1890). Had a draper's shop (almost certainly *the* draper's shop in Ashton). A deacon for twenty-six years, Treasurer of the Chapel and Congregation for eight. Taught in the Sunday School.

Mrs. Wren:

> Esther Ashton, later Mrs. Green. Ran a private school.

Miss Wrigley:

> Miss Ripley, who worked tirelessly for the Sunday Schools for no less than fifty years, from their opening in 1862: Albion Schools Jubilee was hers as well. 'Blessed with long and continuous good health, mental and physical vigour, and a wealth of religious and spiritual zeal, her labours, not only in connection with the Sunday schools, but throughout the entire Congregation, have been alike abundant and fruitful'.

PLACES

Stageport	Stockport
Stallbridge / Mossbridge	Stalybridge
Duckington	Dukinfield
Benton	Denton
Iveley / Mossborough	Mossley
Seeke	Hyde
Ashton-on-the-Hill	Ashton-under-Lyne

I
THE JOY OF LIFE

I DO not believe that life would have been what it was, or the half of what it was, if we had not been the contemporaries of Mr. John Ogden Green. And indeed when I come to think of it that is what as a community and what I may call a culture, we were – the contemporaries of Mr. John Ogden Green. He was a man born for organization, and when I think of him closely, I begin to see that the objects of organization had become quite secondary in his mind to the process itself. Thus, I never heard him expand largely on theology or church government, or express any decided political opinion except personal contempt for the Conservatives, and even this was latent and implied rather than stated. I think it possible indeed that he may have come to regard the Congregational chapel and the Liberal party not as means to some ulterior end, and therefore, *ex hypothesi,* perishable organizations, but as final good in themselves. It is of course a danger with executive minds like his. But if I were called on to bring back the classical and what I may call the golden and Augustan age of Ashton-on-the-Hill, I do not know how I should go on with such an enterprise, for the spirit bloweth where it listeth and they that were born of that strong gust of the spirit are gone, but I should certainly begin with the shop of Mr. Ogden Green in Warrington Street. I should then know how to arrange the scene. Behind the glass door of the shop I should place where it would be visible from the street Mr. Ogden Green's face and long red beard. He is in conversation with a caller in the shop, and is at the moment gazing abstractedly after the tram-car as it sprawls on its way to Mossbridge behind its cavalcade of three horses. It is plain that some question of committee procedure has been raised. The interior of the shop is easy to remember. It was furnished with mahogany shelves bearing rolls of cloth, some of which were overcoatings; some suitings, and others, with equal certitude, only trouserings. A few prints high up above the shelves showed large groups of gentlemen occupied in urbane conversation in Hyde Park, and apparelled in a height of fashion and with a precision of fit and an indentation of crease which represented an ideal rather than an ambition. By day, Mr. Ogden Green was a tailor. By day, and in the intervals of chapel organization!

No matter that it be Monday morning – spiritless, secular, becalmed, unaired time of week – we shall yet perceive around and about the door of Mr. Ogden Green's shop the churned wake of powerful, sectarian steaming the day before.

Mr. John Hills, the organist, has just been in to discuss, all over again, how the singing "went", and Mr. Dillworth has twinkled round the corner from the Overseers' Office, partly to be measured for his new overcoat and partly on a matter of chapel accounts, and Mr. Harkness, the minister, a sensationally delicate man who seldom went out between Sundays except to risk his life at an important funeral, has stepped down from the Manse in his grey muffler and wide-awake to confer on the highest and most private synagogics. Alas! it cannot be again for ever, but I am sure that if I could get Mr. Ogden Green back again behind the glass door of his shop with something important on his mind, all the rest would follow and I should again see the colour and feel the stir of life – opening *soirées* of the Literary Society, which we were beginning just then to call *conversazziones*, choir trips for the day to Dolgelley; temporary closing of Wycliffe Chapel for renovations and repairs; reopening of Wycliffe when it turned out to be a feast of pink and pale green paint and so heavily bedizened in varnish that for five years thereafter the pew-doors cracked like pistol shots as we broke away; titanic bazaars and special efforts of all kinds; rounders in the field on Whit Friday with a powdery and perfectly virginal white ball produced from Mr. Ogden Green's tail-coat pocket; Pontefract cakes passed along the ranks of the choir before and after the anthem for the amelioration of the throat; boiled ham, currant buns, hot coffee, and all the rest. Of such was it to be a contemporary of this remarkable man! I do not believe that the years have shown me anyone since whom it was better worth while to know, or one who added so much to the enrichment of life. I always thought the setting of his days romantic in the extreme. He had two shops. One of them was sacred to crewel or fancy work, and was tended by the vestal women of his household. In the other, he himself measured, cut and fitted the clothes of that ultramontane part of the congregation who encountered him constantly on "executives" and found it a heart-burning thing to meet his eye in a garment he had not made. Having two shops, he had also two houses, which, by the breaking through of doors, had been turned into one vast kosmic interior, hardly smaller as it seemed to me, certainly not less various and climatic than the continents of earth themselves. I declare that Chatsworth can hardly have seemed a larger house. Enjoying his friendship and the run of the house, I must have been one of the very few who could without mistake go by that North-West Passage of back-stairs from the kitchen – the like of which I have not seen since, for the flash of its fender, for tea cakes and strawberry jam, and the violent heat of the cat's fur – to the remote arctic drawing-room which was never lighted except on Sunday. Indeed the light in Mr. Ogden Green's window over the dark shop spoke to me more indubitably than anything else of Sunday as I ran to the post through the darkling streets, with the new-falling snow like elastic beneath the feet and the bell in the church tower ringing a lofty frost-bound tenor.

And then there were unoccupied rooms stacked with green cardboard boxes into any one of which it was worth while to look, and behind the table, at which Mr. Ogden Green "cut" my Eton suits, there was a glass door at which senile men appeared for more stitching, which they carried over their arms by an outside staircase up to a garret. In this garret they sat on the floor like a circle of gnomes in a strong smell of something singeing. Truly a man who lived his life and had everything interesting about him – his periodical sick-headaches were things we were not privileged to behold, but Mrs. Ogden Green, who ministered to them with cold compresses, reported – and in fact it was common talk – that they were phenomenal. They had in fact acquired the standing of kosmic and seasonal things, and were spoken of like the periodic activity of volcanoes or the neap tides. I have heard the chairmen of meetings ask someone else to read the minutes in the absence of Mr. Ogden Green, who was "suffering from one of his sick-headaches".

For indeed his real life was at Wycliffe Chapel. In choir practices! I can see him and indeed hear him blow his nose vehemently before trying the passage again, "Basses alone this time" – how enjoyable it was when he assumed an air of a culprit for the benefit of the much-gratified contraltos! But above all was his real life in the momentous sessions of committees, committees which were "general" or "executive" or, better still, "sub", to say nothing of that special kind of committee which is endowed with the excellent mystery of "power to add to its numbers", or, as Mr. Ogden Green would have put it, "the power to add". And all this being so, he blended better than any man I have ever known with a good Sunday night. I have been with him through Sunday nights which seemed to reach peak after peak of culmination. There was that appetizing moment when Principal This or Doctor That undulated like a cat up the pulpit stairs, contemplating an even greater sermon than that of which he had been delivered in the morning. It seemed, again, like a supreme climax when the forms were being carried shoulder-high out of the aisles to release the regular pew-holders. But there is yet a later period of the same evening with which I always best associate Mr. Ogden Green. He almost always came to our house on Sunday night to supper, and it was while he sat among us with one leg stiffly thrown across the other, that the financial if not the spiritual results of the day were winnowed, sifted and gathered into barns while hymnody and last appeals still burnished the western skies of consciousness. He had the true Dissenting genius for Sunday night, bringing to the table a marked revival of appetite and the subtle aroma of one who had been powerfully behind the scenes. If it had been the day of the "annual sermons" he could tell us what exactly it had cost to have Dr. Parker, and what it would have cost to have had not Dr. Parker but Dr. Dale. Others might know divines by their doctrine; he knew them by their price.

II
THE BIG BAZAAR

IN the inner circles of the congregation, where people talked much in metaphor and imagery, the Bazaar during the long period of its approach ceased to figure in talk as the Bazaar, and was known colloquially and without the need of further particularization as "the great effort". But in many forms of words pictorially and imaginatively conceived, justice was done to the heroic and stupendous size of the undertaking. It was sometimes referred to as "what we had on our hands" or as "what lay before us". The amount which was to be raised was indeed a large one, and only the noticeable percentage among us of "carriage people" made the ambition a practicable one. At the tea-tables of the town it was often said in the course of that summer that at Wycliffe "they have their hands full". The same remark might have been heard among Ashton-on-the-Hill people, knitting or viewing the vacant horizon at the end of Blackpool pier, and if any of Wycliffe was present when this was said, she would smile the faint smile of one who was used to being handled by Destiny – the slightly superior smile proper to those who were accustomed to things on the notoriously big scale of "Wycliffe". When it was over and had settled down into illustrious history, the Bazaar was known for many years as "the Big Bazaar", and one of the most enjoyable and familiar of Mr. Ogden Green's reminiscences was concerned with the germination of the idea which led to so great an event.

Like other big things in our history, it was traceable ultimately to the accident that "a few of us got talking". On this occasion they got talking in the chapel yard after a deacons' meeting – that chapel yard in which a good deal of half-obliterated reading-matter on the flags attests the presence below of a considerable company of the long-since departed. The subject of the talk was the chapel debt. Though considerable in amount and not slightly over-due, the debt was wholly free from that moral taint which attaches to the unpaid bills of individuals. Perhaps the difference was faintly indicated in the words in which they referred to its extinction – it was not so much to be "paid" as to be "wiped out". Moreover, it had been in some rather special and exotic sense of the word "incurred", and, as they talked beneath the gas jet which fought precariously for its life in the draught round the corner of the chapel yard, it was figured as "hanging over" the congregation as though its imminence over the head of the congregation was something for which the congregation was in no sense to blame. In the street outside the chapel yard was the carriage of Mr. Henry

Stonor, at once a deacon of Wycliffe and Member for the borough. It was a definite enrichment of life to everybody in the talk to be familiar with Mr. Stonor, who in turn was distinctly though distantly known to Mr. Gladstone. The talk, at any rate, came to a head at the door of Mr. Stonor's carriage. The moment was favourable for getting something done because the general meeting of the deacons had dissolved half an hour before, and had precipitated into its essential constituents of power and purpose. We were governed by committees, but committees never make history. It is only made by strong men. The door of Mr. Stonor's carriage closed with a snap. His bay horses struck a hoof-full of sparks from the stone sets. The other square-hatted figures separated into the night, and when Mr. Ogden Green half an hour later sat down with the wife of his bosom and the daughters of his house to the coffee and pastry which he had not found in a pretty long life to do him any harm, he announced that "there would probably be a Bazaar".

It tells us something of what that Bazaar had been that for years we were not tired of talking about it. Long after the reminiscence was exhausted in what we may call its scope and rotundity, it could still be discussed with pleasure in detail. Its leaf, as the Psalmist says – its leaf as distinguished from its fruit – never withered. It registered, for example, the high-water mark of "giving", and that, not only in money but in hams and tongues and jellies and cheese-cakes. I believe it to be moreover an historical fact – though I cannot prove it – that it marked the climax and culmination of English needlework. It stood out from others, again, in the size of the sum at which it aimed, but this was only a difference in degree not distinguishing it essentially from the mere "sale of work" which anyone could see it was not. Very exquisite things had been and were indeed done any year for sales of work – things which "it was a sin to let go at a guinea". The real distinction of the big Bazaar lay in the bold and innovating spirit which disclosed itself in the entertainments. In nothing was it shown more signally than in the Tableaux Vivants. The inclusion of the Tableaux Vivants among the entertainments was a striking movement, an approach to the questionable arts of the drama and the stage which probably had its critics, though opposition was not organized, partly because the project introduced itself and made some progress towards preparation under the slightly frigid name of "living statuary". It was in the formulation of ideas for living statuary that Miss Cheeseman, who was known chiefly as an authority on the vicissitudes of the Children of Israel, disclosed an unexpected acquaintance with the more prominent personages of pagan mythology, and when, on the first night, the curtain, after a brief but anguished period of obstinacy, went back and

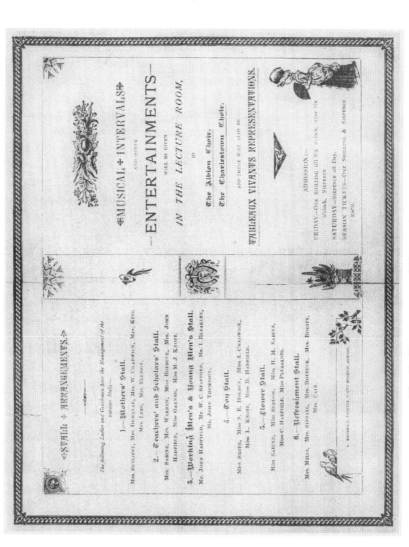

Fig. 3. Programme of Entertainments

exhibited protuberant through a black curtain at various altitudes, a number of heads richly and curiously improved upon with whitening and cotton wool – the whole forming what was obviously and in spite of a marked tendency to blink, a gallery of busts – it was her erudition which had suggested the names of Jupiter, Mercury, Vulcan and the rest, and her fingers which had effected the disguises which for a time baffled the fierce attempts of the spectators at identification. Mr. Fred Space, the solo tenor in the choir, was quickly detected as Mercury, partly by his indifferent success in maintaining his gravity, partly by a length and meagreness of neck which was not a characteristic of that well-favoured deity, and partly by the indifferent adhesiveness of a large and responsible patch of his cotton-wool. Miss Cheeseman herself figured unselfishly as one of the three witches in "Macbeth", and indeed the classical and slightly chilly feeling of the first item passed away as the programme entered upon things more Italian and romantic, and the limelight began to assume the hue of raspberry vinegar. It was the "gipsy encampment" at the end which disclosed with certitude that the nature and proper designation of the entertainment was Tableaux Vivants. In the Bazaar itself the name was bandied about a lot, and those who were not members of the company made much light play with its French and new-fangled character. Mr. Ogden Green, indeed, found the name – pronounced as it is spelled – a piece of agreeable social vivacity in itself. He made a great point of pronouncing it exactly as it is spelled.

But all this was only light froth on the powerful and, by Saturday night, torrential racing of the main stream of the Bazaar. About nine o'clock on that night the Bazaar could be seen to be approaching its Niagara. Admission was now at a price almost negligible, and the family and season-ticket holders were almost swamped by a barbaric invasion from the street. Through great gaps left by departed antimacassars, bedspreads and "work" the Bazaar began to expose the ribs and cross-bones of its skeleton, and in the packed and overheated congestion the girls of the congregation – attended by young men to whom they were by now as good as engaged – were raffling last articles recklessly torn down from the stalls. To book the names of those who "put in" the young men held their pencils high over their heads, and the girls entwined in these partnerships twisted through the crowd, exuding a warm and gushing womanliness. Those who had taken part in the "gipsy encampment" – just presented for the last time though something had been said of an extra performance on Monday – were moving about in full costume and exciting, such was the tension of the moment, hardly any remark. It was known to a select few that Mrs. Scrape, the chapel-keeper's wife, had been severely injured behind the refreshment stall by the neck of a bottle of ginger-beer, and in one of the class-rooms downstairs was receiving first aid from Dr. Macfarlane, whose presence among us at all, indicated the unexampled height to which things had risen, for Dr. Macfarlane, though an undoubted adherent of Wycliffe, was excused by his professional duties from attending public worship, and in point of fact had hardly ever been known to attend except for the funeral service of a patient. But the news relating to Mrs. Scrape did not spread. The Bazaar was dishevelled – contortional and uproarious in its last frenzy – and when Mr. Ogden Green, standing on an inverted "dip" at nearly midnight, gave out the final figures, the "Old English village" was in ruins. But it had served its purpose. The chapel debt, or rather *that* chapel debt, was wiped out.

III
RITUALISTS!

WE were under the impression at Wycliffe Chapel that we were opposed to all ritual. We called it mummery and flummery. Nine-tenths of the religious life consisted in conduct; the other tenth, in sermons. A good choir was an assistance. A satisfactory heating apparatus was an essential – there were no draughts in Wycliffe Chapel. Sunday clothes were, of course, *de rigueur.* Wycliffe Chapel itself was a rectangular building, all brick without and all pitch-pine and varnish within. The steps to its three front entrances were whitened and were in spiritual relationship to the scullery sinks of many members of the congregation. Since we lived in Lancashire, our life was powdered with a light coating of soot, but we objected passionately to organic dirt, and my own mother reserved her judgment of a house and its inhabitants until she had had an opportunity of seeing the scullery. A good scullery sink was one in such a state that you could "eat your dinner from it" should such an extreme emergency arise.

And yet I do not think that Wycliffe Chapel was an unmysterious building. On the contrary, many of its numerous vestries and antechambers were full of romantic interest. I have often been in it alone. There was a certain vestry which housed an immense battalion of tea-urns, and the large organ in the chapel had had a family of small harmoniums, deeply encased in wood but containing a succulent and syrupy kind of music, if you gave them breath with your feet. And then there were the winding wooden stairs which led up to the tempestuous apartment where the organ was "blown". This chamber was on occasion full of sound and wind and fury, and great sporting interest was lent to it by the movement up and down on a wooden panel of a small piece of lead which told the labouring blower how the organ was for wind. In certain choruses from the "Messiah" and in "Onward, Christian Soldiers" this evil spider evinced a strong determination to climb up to the place where someone had drawn a thick line with a black lead pencil and written the laconic word "Empty", and it was an impressive thing to watch the sinister creature and to reflect that only half an inch – and that precariously held – was saving the congregation from the awful disaster of the sudden death of the organ. It would be a mistake to say that Wycliffe Chapel was a prosaic building. On the other hand, it had none of the certificated beauty of stained glass or of stone aisles and prostrate attitudes. To these things we objected – on principle!

Our principal objection to the Parish Church was that its prayers were all in print and that the Rector knew them by heart. This is what we called "vain repetition". We took it moreover as an unmistakable sign of a certain poverty both of language and idea in the Church of England. With us, the ability to pray in public for a sufficient length of time and with an adequate flow of ideas was not only a desirable accomplishment but a necessity to any man who wished to rise to high consequence and to count and shine in affairs. No head of a family could go even to a committee meeting with a guarantee that he would not be asked to "lead us in prayer". The exercise thus went far beyond the devotional meditations of Thomas Cranmer, which did well enough for the Parish Church. Public prayer with us took the form of a spirited and highly topical review of the field of contemporary events, all the more interesting because it was so allusive and oblique. "Did Mr. Harkness", we asked, "preach this morning on the Education Bill". "No", might be the reply, *"but he referred to it in his prayer".*

That was indeed the exact difference of literary treatment. Things were said in sermons or addresses, while references were made in prayers. It was understood that God had read the *Manchester Guardian* that morning, and it was a sign of intelligence among the company of bowed heads to be able to "pick up" allusions either to congregational events like the approaching bazaar, which would figure as "the great effort which is before us", or as to public happenings like – for example – the death of Cardinal Newman, whose high place in our esteem was an example of a man's life being greater after all than his creed. Cardinal Newman would enter into a prayer as "that other servant of Thine who is not of our fold". On the other hand, Mr. Gladstone – who was also, by the way, a clerically minded man and not of our flock – was so majestic and elemental that his name was not always even paraphrased, and I have heard him named by his name with abrupt and dramatic effect – "We pray Thee to bless and sustain Mr. Gladstone". One of our chapel statesmen who was both frequent and fluent in prayer, feeling it necessary to allude to an illness which was being undergone at the time by Dr. Parker, described the sufferer as "Thy servant who is now lying ill in the principal city of our land". This localization of Dr. Parker's sufferings was felt by the intellectuals who were present to be an approach to banality and bathos. I cannot agree with this. It certainly rounded the sentence. Moreover, it added to the impressiveness of the affair that it was taking place not in a hole and corner but on a stage where things were always on a big scale. Besides, it was necessary to identify Dr. Parker beyond possibility of mistake. There might have been a famous Congregationalist ill at Wolverhampton!

And yet we had emancipated ourselves from the rubric of the Parish Church only to fall victims to another one of our own making. New presbyter was but old priest writ large, and in doing things exactly as we had always known them done, I have never known such sticklers as we. There were houses among us in which it was a point of something more even than honour, a point of definite morals, not to be "late for chapel". "Chapel" began at half-past ten, and there was a quality and value – a virtue somehow – in half-past ten which was not in eleven. It was a moment having a certain blessedness to itself, and, though we knew by our own experience of seaside places and by report of the South of England, that it was a custom even among some congregations of the elect to begin at eleven, and even more eccentrically at a quarter to eleven, we never quite lost a sense of pity for the South of England that this should be so. There was one family at least among us with whom it was a precision to be late by the exact length of the first hymn and prayer. They were not among our most important people, but this peculiarity made them famous. Sunday after Sunday they mis-measured it to the moment, shouldering up the aisle powerfully, a numerous and accurately graded family, and just as we were proceeding from what had gone before to "hymn number one hundred and fifty" – to be found with equal certitude as "the hundred and fiftieth hymn" just as we were finding it in our books, it always occurred to the moment – the draught along the aisle as the Lawsons entered and advanced, the admission of a capful of the unregenerate Sabbath-breaking weather outside, the roar of their progress along the drugget, the angry retort of the ventilation grid as Mr. Lawson, who came last, spurned it with his heel.

And there was a mind in whose decisions I was much concerned myself, which could never be brought to see that if I put three separate copper pennies in the collection-box the result both to me and the missions – Home, Foreign, or, for that matter, Church Aid – was precisely the same as if I had put in a threepenny-bit. It might be true – but what is truth? – and arguments directed to establish it were firmly trodden down and were indeed, as I can see now, the idlest sophistry. It was in vain that I fell back on the ultimate contention that the box was so carpentered that no one could see what one put in it, or for that matter – with a little pantomime – whether one put anything in at all. She had "never been accustomed to give copper", and I believe that rather than deposit a family of secular coppers on the green lining of that box she would have borne the unheard-of shame of waving it past her altogether. Silver was ritual – her two-shilling piece and my threepenny-bit. It was canon and rubric. It was more than that, because it was decreed by real Infallibility – by her to herself.

Not ritualists, indeed! I have a distinct sense of having come back to consciousness every Sunday morning in a sort of eastward position. Sunday must have begun very early, for I never wakened when it was due but it was already there, come up like a tide in the night out of the unexplorable depths, out of the history if not the nature of things, palpable in the garden, visible in the arrested breathing of the chimneys across the valley, in the meek deportment of the poultry in the field – the world full to the brim of Sunday! And I can yet feel the still sobriety of its early hours, the conversation of the sparrows in the roof, the sonorousness of a distant chanticleer, the occurrence of a milk-cart far along the road, the thrust of pale sunbeams as the window-blind stirred, the early communings of the window-blind with itself. And there was the excursion to the distant downstairs for the clothes which had been "airing" in the cupboard, and on the kitchen hearthrug the cat, built up like a buttress, and absorbed in exceptional and far-reaching ablutions, as though it also knew the influence and confessed the hour. That kitchen fender itself, polished to the quick of its being, spiritualized almost away by much suffering from Bath brick, was itself an altar at which no detail in the appointed ceremony of the day would be foregone.

Later in the day, when we came back from Wycliffe Chapel, it would carry a load of plates, plates in two sizes for the two courses, the greater which went before, and the lesser which never failed to come after. And then someone would come in and would ask "how the singing had gone", the singing being notoriously a very temperamental thing, and someone else, just returned from her religious exercises, would ask us all whether we had noticed Mrs. Fentem's new bonnet - "*Did* you see Mrs. Fentem's new bonnet?" She would add that she, for her part, had never seen anything like it, and then some doubt would arise whether it was a new bonnet or an ancient architecture restored but still recognizable - in short, Mrs. Fentem's old bonnet "done up".

Our attitudes at Wycliffe were not those of stained glass, and Mr. Darlington's attitude towards the second, which was also the longer and more intimate prayer, though it might have been worthily done in cast-iron, could never have been rendered in crewels or silk. Mr. Darlington, who stood up to Mr. Gladstone on Home Rule, also stood erect and monumental through all the prayers. In the first prayer he had companions. Other heads of families had this same habit of communing with the Lord erect and unafraid. But the second prayer was a longer prayer, and through this he stood alone, a single tall trunk shooting up supervisory from a prairie of crouching under growth. And we had our "moments" too – not at St. Peter's or St. Paul's, I think, can one moment have signified more than another. There was the moment when the organist climbed back on to his seat and began selecting stops. It was a sure intimation that the sermon was round the corner and on the last lap home. Never – such was the skill that had come of long gauging and such the advantage of being able to overlook the orator's notes on the pulpit ledge – had he been known to miscalculate or spread the tidings seriously or blameably too soon. And there was the sense of easing off which came with the collection. The belated arrival of the collector from a remote and populous gallery, his startling and solitary tread audible down invisible staircases and then in full view along the aisle, marked the end of the collection. We sat and waited for him while the organist improvised. I used to imagine that public life held no ordeal more terrible than that of the collector who had the distant and populous gallery, and who got home, solitary and belated, treading the inflamed silences with squeaky boots. Yes, we had our ritual!

IV
CARNIVAL

AN expert could have predicted the exact moment when Whitsuntide would break out; he could have specified the place from which it would be best visible, and, just as astronomers who expect a comet are never kept waiting, however long ahead the appointment is made, so too the moment Whitsuntide would have occurred. The moment of its occurrence was two o'clock in the afternoon – on Whit-Sunday.

At that moment in one of our long streets of what they call "cottage property", where some of the front doorsteps are stoned the colour of Cochin China eggs and some are stoned white, where bamboo tripods supporting bronze flower-pots are invariable between the curtains, and Dickens, Disraeli or Gladstone glare from the fanlight, a door would open and a bevy of small children, resplendently dressed but carrying themselves with a precision and anxiety which do not go with the similar plumage of kingfishers, and betraying indeed in some instances traces of a recent tearfulness, would emerge.

They would turn their faces in the direction of Wycliffe Sunday School, but the departure would not be managed without certain drastic and even vicious last touches on the doorstep, nor without advice given in a louder key than could be nice for those whose self-consciousness was already extreme. "Now, 'Arold, mind what th'art about", and 'Arold, who was condemned for the next twelve months to appear on all public occasions as a chieftain of the Seaforth Highlanders – the decision having been arrived at to apparel him in kilts – would proceed to mind what he was about, it being the easier to do so from the circumstance that his boots were new and he was not sure that one of them did not pinch. 'Arold might, in fact, indicate at least half a mind to begin blubbering, but by this time other doors in the same street were opening and letting out similar tricklings of finery, and he would catch the spirit of the thing and would become absorbed in the transfiguration of familiar acquaintances.

It was Carnival. The Venetians and the Neapolitans run the streets crying Carnival. Mary Hannah and Joseph Henry – "our Mary Hannah" and "our Joseph Henry" – meant the same thing, but they walked, walked with tentative and talkative steps and as though the world were all wet paint, and Mary Hannah, feeling what seemed like a bump of rain among the marguerites on her hat, seized Joseph Henry by the wrist and hurried him on, wondering whether she ought to spread a knotted pocket-handkerchief on her hat. They were near

Wycliffe by now – no longer "our Mary Hannah" and "our Joseph Henry" but units in one of several brilliant processions which were converging on the open doors and stone staircases of Wycliffe Sunday School.

Wycliffe received itself on Whit-Sunday afternoon with a roar of gratification. No attempt was made, as it would be made in other societies, to address oneself to the eyes of a distant acquaintance and to ignore his new clothes. Everybody – except the teachers who were drawn from the higher strata of the congregation in which wardrobes were renovated at any odd time of the year – invited criticism and would indeed have been offended if it had been suppressed. The late arrival of striking conceptions in lilac or crushed strawberry would cause a large acreage of the school to stampede to its feet. In some families they got a kind of cumulative effect, and sisters would appear duplicated so exactly that there seemed no reason why the eyes of the Young Men's First Class should choose the one and leave the other, or why for two such twin berries, life should have two purposes and two destinies which were not the same. And when at last the Superintendents had got order by importunate stampings on the cracked bell, the assembled school of Wycliffe spread itself like a June flower-bed in the Corporation Park.

But all aristocracies are comparative. From the doors of small and evil-smelling tenements which elbowed the architecture of the school and peered over the playground with the swings, the tricklings of finery had been surveyed by others who were not going to school and who had literally, as society ladies generally have figuratively, "nothing to go in". In these houses the flag had been hauled down. The point of greatest pride in Lancashire had been surrendered, and the children of those houses eyed the assembling of Wycliffe stoically - taking it fatalistically as youth can and does.

*   *   *

In Ashton-on-the-Hill we "walked" on Whit-Friday and had done so immemorially. "Walked" was the chosen word for what we did on that day, and it seems strange that in such humble and unpretentious fashion we should have described our progress through the public streets, two by two, between lines of spectators, behind banners and bands of music, in a state of intense consciousness both of self and schism. I have said "schism" because the proceedings of the day were indeed frankly and unblushingly sectarian. We who were Dissenters "walked" in the morning. It was not a convenient arrangement, but we accepted it because the Church had seized the afternoon. In the morning, consequently, Dissent was between the tram-lines and Church was on the pavement. In the afternoon it was Dissent on the pavement and Church between the tram-lines, and in the course of the completed day each had examined the other with considerable interest both qualitatively and quantitatively. It is to be remembered again that those who were Dissenters, dissented on different grounds and from different aspects of doctrine. Over the whole expounded scheme of creation, fall and redemption, hardly a single proposition had been laid down, from which somebody in Ashton-on-the-Hill had not dissented and found others to dissent with him. There were several "bodies" among us having church buildings, church membership and church finance which had shot up out of the interpretation of single verses of the New Testament – like plants out of plant pots. They all "walked" on Whit-Friday and they all "walked" separately, crossing one another at right angles and obtuse angles like caterpillars on a cabbage leaf. Our local Christendom was not re-united; did not want to be. Every year there occurred a moment at which in one of our meaner streets we "met the Catholics" face to face. Though inferior to us in numbers and of course deeply mistaken in all their views, they were undoubtedly a nicer and a nobler spectacle than we. Conscious as I was, that the part of the procession in which I figured lacked both colour and interest, I often raised a question as to this superior appearance of Catholics when in public procession, but was told that it was the kind of thing "they ought to be good at". The answer was a dark hint that they were not particularly good at anything else, and the worst heresy of all was nipped in the bud.

This was what the day was like. It was therefore one of the revelations of the after years that Whit-Friday was not Whit-Friday everywhere; not kosmic and not even common. It was in fact only later that I came to know that elsewhere on this day the pulse of England was normal and its face calm – that Carter Paterson vans were sliding as usual down the slope of Chancery Lane into the Strand; that in the High Streets of Southern towns the butcher's pony meditated most of the morning opposite the shop-door, untroubled by brass bands; that in the broad shires farmers' wives in their traps waited for gates and level crossings to unclose. Every genuine Lancashire man who has left Lancashire must have felt himself chilled and contracted by these discoveries.

And yet I once got a momentary suspicion that in the vague outside the wagging of the world was unstayed. It was when I was sent to the station to meet Mrs. Wren. Mrs. Wren had kept a highly select school in the town until she married and went to live at a nicer place on the coast. It was on Whit-Friday that she intimated to Ashton-on-the-Hill that she still remembered and understood. She used to sit over the signboard of the fancy shop of Mr. Ogden Green and survey the procession through a pair of gold spectacles wide and placid as evening window-panes. Her presence at the window of Mr. Ogden Green caused among the "gentlemen of the congregation" who headed the procession – representing all that was best and most eminent in the town in accountancy and cotton-waste – the exposure of numerous unexpectedly bald heads. At dinner afterwards, she would tell us who was still "keeping wonderfully young" and who was "failing". It seldom happened that there was not someone whom Mrs. Wren certified to be "failing fast". I have known no one with a more tranquil acceptance of the mortality of man.

The day that I was sent to meet Mrs. Wren at the station a North-Western train suddenly occurred at the curved platform. The passengers studiously ignored Ashton-on-the-Hill, and when I saw the guard move a bag of letters an inch or two on the platform with his foot, and then catch the eye of the driver along the train, I suffered a momentary slip in my perspective of things, and the chilling thought struck me that the storm was all in a tea-cup. But the thought did not last. I urged Mrs. Wren on, telling her that the band had already gone up to the school.

I do not think we were a processionally minded race, and as a mere spectacle we were open to some aesthetic criticism. We were not good at "keeping up" and were thus apt to let daylight be seen through gaps in our continuity. To fill these gaps we resorted to undisguised and confessed running or rather rapid trickling, in which teachers urged us on by a rather more open display of discipline than was seemly before all and sundry in the streets. Many of us could only keep our stockings up by repeated re-application to the problem, and the procession generally was open to the objection that the best wine came first, and after it that which was worse. The band came first, and after the band the blue silk banner, causing titanic suffering to the men who carried it in sockets slung around their necks. Grouped around the banner was a remarkable assemblage of eminence and beauty. It consisted of the "gentlemen of the congregation", monumental and Olympian, and around them a cluster of our younger virgins, their dresses white, their hats trimmed with marguerites, their chins deeply indented with new elastic which would be loosened a little with the scissors before the next time of doing service. There was nothing like this in the rest of the procession. It degenerated steadily, and at any given point where I myself arrived among the smaller boys, I usually found the spectators thawing away or at any rate manifesting little either of admiration or enthusiasm.

After a time I fear we ceased to be consciously processional at all, and that our walking became a definitely business-like and somewhat urgent errand to the field where we might expect refreshments. At the posts of the gate through which we filtered at last into the field, were the two baskets fathoms deep in buns, and over each basket toiled a heated, preoccupied, man. Into each hand as it passed he thrust one of the buns. It was no time for the excusing of fingers, and, though one might know him in private life and at moments of greater leisure quite well, one received no recognition. We had ceased to be individuals, and were the mere receptacles of buns. To have refused a bun would have been a departure from etiquette and even decency. Even Mr. Harkness, our minister, who had walked in the procession immediately behind the blue silk banner and whose hat had scarcely been on his head since the moment of stepping out – such was his eminence in the town – received a bun with full geniality. Nevertheless, it was still possible to indicate some social eclecticism in the handling and management of one's bun. It was certainly the thing in our set to treat it with some measure of detachment, to break a piece off and thus approach it delicately by an advance on its flank, rather than attack it by direct dental assault, and above all to manifest an early satiety – to take it, in fact, as an incident in the ritual of the day, sacramentally rather than as sheer nourishment. And besides this, the bun itself put up some resistance because it was supplied without any liquid facilitation, and though lemonade was to be had in mugs, it was not free. Miss Cheeseman, who had advanced to the field at the head of her own senior class for girls, used to hand her bun almost in its integrity to any contiguous small boy, and seemed to regret the attachment which springs up between baked sugar and grey kid gloves. But the warm aroma of those buns used to hang like a curtain around the gate-posts into the field. It mingled with the smell of the trodden grass.

It was in the improvised sports of the field that Mr. Ogden Green proved himself every year no mean athlete. A game of rounders was always constituted on the outskirts of the general revels. Mr. Ogden Green had a passion for rounders. It is a game requiring but a modest equipment, but a ball is necessary and it was always Mr. Ogden Green who produced the ball. And, indeed, I have never known that far-sighted man to set out on any open-air expedition, whether it was the WhitFriday procession or a picnic to the Corporation Waterworks, but his figure was compromised by his having somewhere about him a ball, milk-white and virginal to the eye, agreeably pungent to the nose and dusted with a white powder delectable as the bloom upon the grape. It was a challenge to rounders when he dived into his tail-coat pocket, produced such a ball with a final wrench and threw it provocatively on the ground. In the game which always followed, many of the players were congregationally eminent. The rustle of Miss Cheeseman's cloth dress as she ran from one walking-stick to the next, and thence to the "den", was like a breeze among the larger branches of the trees, and the habitual restiveness of Mr. Ogden Green's neck within the grip of his collar – a noticeable peculiarity even when he was at repose – was now greatly aggravated by heat and enthusiasm and became a sensational peculiarity. And then singly and in groups we fell away from the game. I think the evening of Whit Friday fell very flat in Ashton-on-the-Hill. I have known it to rain, and both the house and the garden were full of unaerated twilight. Uneasy are the wanderings of those who are still dressed up but have nowhere else to go.

V
THE DEATH OF HENRY STONOR

EVERYBODY lowered his voice and everybody got nearer to somebody else when the news flew over the town that Mr. Stonor was going to die. The news did not take quite so definite and precise a form as that; it went no further for the present than to say that Mr. Stonor was "worse". "Have you heard", we asked one another, "that Mr. Stonor is worse?" Though this need not have been decisive, it somehow was. Some who heard it for the first time had the presence of mind to be "not at all surprised", and by being "not at all surprised" they scrambled back on to equal conversational terms almost in the moment of being pushed off. Less agile spirits accepted the news tractably and said, "Ee dear, they had not heard"; but all, however they took it, indicated that their minds were on the instant satisfactorily sealed against all possible hope. "Mr. Stonor – worse". It was characteristic of that tremendous citizen that he had never promised but he had also performed.

It had always been so. It was so when he said that the anniversary sermons must yield the unheard-of sum of two hundred and fifty pounds on the day's collections, and so also when he said that the new refreshment-room on the railway station, frequented, it appeared, by the odds and ends of our citizenship who were not going anywhere by train, must be closed – he was a director, and closed it was. And when he said that our young men must give up the tobacco habit on the ground that it had never been necessary to him – for a time and in public they did. We knew that for several days back he had been detained in the big house behind the plane trees with something or other that was seated rather deep, and now it had got about that he was "worse" – no more than that, but enough! Those who got the information in the main street carried it home as though they were carrying something that would break. They experimented on the way with the alternative forms which the announcement might take, so that the news should have its full effect, but nothing was more dramatic than to say curtly that Mr. Stonor was "worse", and having said that, to ask whether supper was ready one could depend with certitude on being plied for the details.

And there were details, plenty of them and corroborative ones. An almost legendary doctor, one who had been knighted by the Queen and was known the length and breadth of the land to consume a tumbler of hot water every morning before his own breakfast, and to be in favour of China tea, had arrived in Ashton-on-the-Hill just when it was going dark. He had beyond doubt

21

Fig. 5. Hugh Mason, M.P. (1817-1886)
'Mr Henry Stonor'
Photo by Elliott & Fry
(from *The Congregationalist*, October 1880)

Fig. 4. Rev. John Hutchison (1824-1899)
'Mr Harkness'
Photo by Lafosse, Manchester
(from *The Congregationalist*, April 1884)

"caught the connection at Stageport", and at the top of the windy flight of wooden stairs into the street a carriage was waiting for him, and in this carriage, with two men in fur capes on the box, though with only one horse in the shafts, the great man had driven swiftly through our streets to Granite Hall; his eyes had looked upon our gas-lights and had seen the nightly drifting to and fro of "the hands". There had been very few illnesses among us that had been dignified by the arrival of a "physician", and I do not know how the great man from Harley Street would have taken it had he known that his visit was an intimation acted on by the entire community to abandon all hope.

What had passed between him and Mr. Stonor we knew not; it had been eminence meeting eminence at a solemn moment of time – eminence on its back and eminence still on its legs – and the subject was one of which imagination might make any historical painting it liked, but it was certain that he had not stayed very long; that the same carriage had driven him an hour later the seven miles or so into Manchester, where we lost him among main lines and termini. The great sweep of his journeyings was talked of all over the town – that and the probable enormity of his fee. Once again Mr. Stonor had made us men of the greater world. We lived the spacious life through him – vicariously. It was he who went into Parliament and took a town house in Onslow Square. And now this illness and the physician coming out of the illustrious void and going back into it – our gas lamps shining meekly into the deep absorptions of his eyes as he drove fast as four legs could carry him through our wet and shiny street! And the next morning we knew that it was all over. We crossed over the street to tell one another that Mr. Stonor "was gone", and wherever two were gathered together in Ashton-on-the-Hill that day they became three. It was agreed that the funeral would be on a large scale.

Life has cost me many illusions, but there has been nothing like the shrinkage of Mr. Henry Stonor into his actual size. I know him now for what in life he never seemed to be. I know now that he was a capitalist with the accent on the "pit". The social economists have got him like a dried specimen in entomology, and right through those fiery vitals of his there is now a systematic pin. It is demonstrable that he was of the Manchester School, a social phenomenon traceable directly to the accident that James Watt watched his mother's kettle boil; that he bought in the cheapest and sold in the dearest market, and that it was the foolish delusion of his breast that the cardinal virtues, if given the chance, would infallibly do for all men what they had done for him. One remembers that bishops caused him a greater degree of grim amusement than any bishop could hope to excite nowadays, and that he thought the disestablishment (not forgetting also the disendowment) of the Church would go further than we now think it would to put the world right – it was one of several things he promised himself he would "live to see". And I know now that Granite Hall was not Olympia but merely a large detached house, and that the drive from the gates to the front door was deliberately twisted so that a little might seem to go a long way. The choir had not infrequently been there to supper, and the leader of the sopranos, who sat at his right hand, told how he waxed playful in the serving of a petulant and self-willed blancmange – how he had followed it on to her lap with a spoon and had humorously pretended to be afraid lest Mrs. Stonor should see what had occurred. As a treat for the senses the funeral was not comparable with that of a sergeant of the Volunteers which had preceded it by a few weeks to the cemetery up the hill. But it was a sensationally long funeral – a centipede among the organisms of fewer legs which crept several times a day along that road which led to nowhere else. Before it took shape, Ashton-on-the-Hill was black with deputations, and their dispersal afterwards was like the rising of a field full of rooks. Nor was the day without its unrehearsed effects, and when once, long afterwards, I saw the fell and awful spectacle of constabulary down among the feet of an insurgent population, my mind went back to the passing of Henry Stonor and the fight at the cemetery gates to get him through to his rest. Mr. Fred Space, the accountant's clerk, was among the unauthorized mourners. He represented nothing but his own curiosity, and was removed at the last moment from a neighbouring tombstone which promised an advantageous view. But, having one foot at least in the door which led to great affairs, he got a glimpse of the will and jotted down the securities on his cuff. They read like a list brought down from Sinai – they constituted, in Mr. Space's opinion, indisputably *the* thing in investments.

VI
THE CLOISTERS

TO our right as we sat arrayed in Wycliffe Chapel there was a row of six large windows. They looked out into the precincts or cloisters of Wycliffe - though I think we called it the chapel-yard. The glass of these six windows was frosted but there must have been a transparent edging or border which was probably pink – such details escape one, but I distinctly remember the partial and occasional visibility of material for a more secular entertainment in the chapel-yard than the matter on which we were met. Small boys, who were as yet imperfectly knit into the close Sunday pattern of school and chapel and school again, and enjoyed a dispensation from the sermon on the ground mainly of St. Vitus's dance, have been known to delay themselves on their way to nowhere in particular outside these windows and to flatten their noses into pools – lakes even when the pressure exerted was strong in the endeavour to see inside, unconscious that we could see them better and even more unfavourably than they could see us. And if anyone fainted, and was removed from our midst, we could, even after the last ripple from the event had died away and the surface was again still, perceive through these windows the enjoyable activity of those who had been entitled, either by relationship or mere officiousness, to accompany the case outside and now had it in hand. And then there was that series of Sundays which occurred between the first appointment of a new choirmaster and the acquirement by that functionary of the right congregational spirit. He thought – bless him – that he had been engaged as a vocalist, and every Sunday morning when the text was given out and it became a question of words and names and of our law, he would be no judge of such matters. He was Gallio, and from his position of extreme prominence, he beat a leisurely and cynical retreat – stepping high over the legs of a row of much-abashed basses – and having disappeared from our much-scandalized view was believed also on the hesitating evidence of the frosted windows, to be promenading in the chapel-yard until such time as the singing was timed to begin again. The process of domesticating him took a little time, but it was eventually achieved, and though his upbringing had been a cathedral one, he became a very earnest man.

The chapel-keeper, again, disturbed from time to time the perfect stillness of the chapel yard. But then the restiveness – the new boots – of the chapel-keeper were always on the fringe of our devotions and nobody marked him. His connection with the Pauline theology was a strictly official one – he had so to speak got above the Word by ministering unto it, and was reserved from the dispensation to which I for instance was subject, of sitting still. He was entitled and was indeed paid to fidget. At any rate, I used to think that a life so full of good excuses, such hatless errands out into the weather, such adventures in the cellar with the heating apparatus, such frolics – if he ever frolicked – in empty vestries where we could not see him, was both an enjoyable and a romantic one. In private conversation, into which indeed he did not enter readily or unreservedly with boys, I never could get Mr. Rhodes to see his life from this aspect. I do not think it had ever occurred to him that he was a chartered libertine – I think he thought it all very plain prose, and indeed the bird outside on the window-sill always does. It is the bird in the cage that thinks it must be so romantic out on the sill.

I do not suppose I should myself have known how intensely exciting a place Wycliffe Chapel was – how it exuded temperament, and was steeped in rich and recognizable smells; how much it had the genius of being full and still more of being empty – if I had not been sent there so often on Sunday afternoons for a certain pair of spectacles which, after careful investigation of several flounces and pleats and an exhaustive review of the hearthrug, the kitchen scales and all other likely places, were finally and truthfully supposed to have been left in chapel in the pew. It was by taking advantage of these opportunities that I performed the operation of removing most of the green baize in the book-box of that pew. I had given some attention to this green baize during the regular hours of Divine service. It was deeply embedded in paint, and came away beautifully like a poultice, but the work at such times was liable to interruption and could not be pursued in peace. But when I was fetching the spectacles I got on with it better, and afterwards I tried various people's places, and marvelled greatly to find how different all their lives their point of view had been from mine. I have been in the pew of Mr. Henry Stonor, which was the backest of back pews, have sat in the shadowy place where we felt rather than saw him to be, and have noted that whereas our pew fitted us like a socket, his was two long paces – a walk in fact – from the back to the front, while cushions with a bloom like grapes, muffs for the feet, big print and a tearful mural tablet up above indicated the very highest and most exclusive realms of faith and of works. I did not know whether such things were of him or his Maker.

Not everyone could have gone straight and infallibly to those spectacles as I was able to go. The way was tortuous and obscure across the chapel-yard and over a sparse colony of graves, through doors which slammed after one as though they would never open again, and by many turnings and twistings of the path through a labyrinth of vestries. I would indeed have been prepared to divide Wycliffe congregation into two well-defined classes of chalk and of cheese by the test of knowing or not knowing the back way in. There were those among us who had always gone in – and come out – by one of the three front doors in Wycliffe Street. These were those of whom we said vaguely that "they had sittings"; those who were with us but not of us – they included the pale and unsalient company of the "oncers". It is not by being so, that one shall smell the cedars of Lebanon, or get into one's nostrils that slightly bitter scent compounded of varnish and hymn-books and cold tea-urns which is as sensuous of Dissent as incense is sensuous of Rome. And those who would pass the test would include all contraltos who inquired of us in a hopeless manner wherewithal a young man might cleanse his way, all basses who certified in unison that lions are apt to lack and suffer hunger, ultramontanes who cut out Union calico for Dorcas meetings and could lay down the law without removing a mouthful of pins, financiers who counted collections and those who habitually read the minutes of the last meeting – and, in short, all who led the life.

Miss Wrigley was one who knew the back way in. Often, indeed, when I have been exploring Wycliffe on those tingling Sunday afternoons I have not been quite alone. It was the singular habit of Miss Wrigley to come more than an hour too soon, and sometimes I have seen her in her close-shuttered bonnet like a solitary rook in an empty field – alone in her place, when nothing was going on but her own thoughts. And it is because of her and others that I have known and are now gone, that I would have liked to call that chapel-yard by the name of the Cloisters. Even though the brick was grimy and the graves powdered with soot; even though the air was vibrant with the perpetual E flat of a cotton-mill and someone passed along the street with a loose iron to his clog; and yet again, though washing was visible in someone's back yard, and the cold-water tap in the corner dripped with a perpetual influenza cold – even so, the Cloisters! For if one knows how to look, all these things will fade away; but the spirit, which is the only real thing – that will not fade away.

VII
ON HAVING SEEN IRVING

THERE was a small minority in our circle in Ashton-on-the-Hill who had seen Henry Irving. There was also one undoubted instance of a visit to a music-hall. This visit to a music-hall – a solitary and sensational occurrence – had happened, of all people, to Mr. Jacob Space, and was one of several glimpses into life, a general enlargement of experience, a sort of compulsory broadening or rather stretching of the mind, which he owed to the circumstance that his second son had embraced the medical profession, and was preparing for it in the most liberal spirit in London. On the night when Mr. Space was introduced to a music-hall by the son who was a medical student, a humorous singer – so at least it leaked out among us – deviated into an account of the domestic arrangements which might be presumed to have obtained "when Noah hung out in the Ark", treating the topic – which though thus offensively introduced, is not, it must be admitted, an incurious one – in so emancipated, candid and searching a spirit and with such a freedom from theological prepossessions, that Mr. Space left the building in considerable dudgeon, followed by his son, who had been bearing it with remarkable equanimity considering the block of which he was a chip. This affair, among those who knew about it, was universally agreed to have been an accident which might have happened to any man in the circumstances.

There was, however, that small minority who had deliberately seen Henry Irving. It must have been an impressive assertion of independence, a notable aspect of the emancipation which came of being grown up – and away from home – and, in short, a bold and questionable thing to do, because I can distinctly recall all the confessions I ever overheard among adult, experienced and widely travelled men of having "been to see Henry Irving" generally in "The Bells". Like the unspeakable thing which happened to Mr. Space, this also had always occurred in the course of visits to London, and the allusion to it was slipped into an interstice of the traveller's narrative – his Odyssey – cropping up, so to speak, between a minute examination of the order of service at Spurgeon's Tabernacle, an account of a narrow shave of seeing Mr. Gladstone at Euston, and regrets at not having been able to get so far as Clapham Common to hear Dr. Guinness Rogers. Even so, I can remember the slight but perceptible change of atmosphere, the touch of blight, the swift modulation from cordiality to politeness – and how shall I call it? – the glimpse down a volcanic crack in the surface, which was opened by this passage of reminiscence. It was somehow implied all round the table, and particularly at the top and bottom of the table, that such a thing would not have been likely to occur anywhere except in London. And so treated the incident brought out more clearly than anything else in the narrative the undoubted physiographical difference between London and Ashton-on-the-Hill – a different latitude, a different temperature and vegetation, and almost, as we now saw, a different Decalogue.

And yet there was much in London that we felt we could understand! We also were a civilization. It was not long before, that a card of invitation had gone forth among us bearing in its left-hand corner, where they were at first overlooked, the four letters R.S.V.P., and though it had been, when it first occurred, a mark of superior attainment calmly and without panic to interpret them, it was now universally understood among us that this was French. In the same spirit, though we were palpably and visibly at home for all the year except a fortnight, we had lately taken to being "at home" in a technical, special, and initiate sense once a month, and had ransacked the calendar like a rag-bag for its "second Tuesdays" and its "third Wednesdays", nearly everybody having carried one off. I myself knew by exploration of a certain drawer in which, besides numerous yards of lace, several dress-lengths which would or would not some day be made up, a best umbrella in a suit of American cloth, plush satchels and a powerful smell of camphor, there was an engraved copper plate wherefrom, at any moment, fresh supplies of visiting cards could be cast, a thing of great atmosphere, mystery and social *sang-froid*, wrapped in tissue paper and testifying to the high complexity and polish of the society in which our elders moved and had their being. Yes, we also were a civilization various and splendid! But Henry Irving! The Lyceum! "The Bells" – or was it "The Lyons Mail"? At any rate, the name occurring amid the tonics of Gladstone and Tennyson and Spurgeon and Parker – occurring warm, seductive and exotic, was like a waft from off a distant perfumed and feverish shore. We could smell it as the travellers can smell Africa.

And of such was the Nonconformist conscience of the middle 'eighties. I remember well the day when it was confronted with Sanger's Circus. The visit of the circus had been the topic of conversation ever since an advertisement in the local paper announced its descent upon the town "for one day only", and catalogued certain items in the programme which were of sensational interest. The editor of the paper was stirred by the prospect to the point of devoting an editorial to the spectacle, which one gathered he had not infrequently seen, and he recommended it to his readers, less initiated and travelled, in warm terms. It was even hinted that the proprietor of the circus was a man of exalted rank, and that his association with any circus at all was a very striking departure from the usual habits of a ducal family, and somehow this was made to serve as a further guarantee of the excellence of the show, though I cannot remember how the argument proceeded.

This was all very well; but the editor did not glance at and still less did he settle the acute question which the imminence of the circus had raised as to the propriety of circuses as a spectacle for the eyes of youth. The Church was generally tolerant of the circus, but Chapel decided, with few dissentients, that there was no place for circuses in its ethical scheme. I belonged myself to Chapel and I deeply deplored the wrong-headedness of my elders, though I took care in the company of Church boys to defend the decision and associate myself with it by various remarks depreciatory of the whole affair. But not even on a moral question in the 'eighties could we have a question of absolute "Aye" or "No". Gradually a compromise was evolved, and we had it canonically laid down that while the proceedings within the tent were not to be encouraged, there could be no harm in any citizen about his business in the town, and, more to the point, any boy returning from school, pausing to see the procession go by and even detaining himself for a space if its arrival was imminent.

And so, accordingly, we saw it enter the town, approaching us in superb processional order along the road from Yorkshire, a rich and spirited cavalcade headed by a dozen ladies on patchy ponies, each pony with a groom at its head. These ladies wore the ordinary riding-habit of the Park, and each one had tilted her silk hat almost to the bridge of a proud and sensitive nose. The contrast between the austerity of the costume and the richness of the complexion, together with the slightly metallic yellow of the profuse back hair, was in the example of each lady marked and arresting. There followed more ladies very questionably dressed, reclining on flat tables spread upon the backs of silky and docile steeds. A college of clowns came next, comporting themselves so as to give some hint of the lengths to which they might be expected to go in the humorous treatment of life when really performing at night; and then there was a miscellaneous zoological collection, brought up finally by a figure of Britannia. She sat aloof and absorbed on a pyramidical structure drawn by more piebald ponies than I had thought the world contained. From her exalted seat she might have taken stock as she came along – if indeed dramatic propriety had not required her to look neither to the right nor left – of the bedroom furniture of a considerable section of the population of Lancashire and Yorkshire, and in her hands she held a trident which heliographed in the morning sun spasmodically. She made a powerful impression on my own mind as the most admirable and attractive human being I had yet beheld, and threw into instant and dismal eclipse one of the contraltos in the choir, of whom till that moment I had thought a good deal.

Though I was forbidden the circus, I lurked a good deal in the course of the evening in its vicinity in the market-place, and I found it possible, by lifting up a yard of canvas, to see rows of pendulous feet and the backs of the multitude strained to a sharp curve in the stress of concentration. I could hear also the thud of hoofs on the tan, and the high-pitched remonstrances of the clowns. I could also hear the band, though that indeed was audible over a considerable circumference, being richly equipped in instruments of brass and percussion. But I do not think that as I knelt with the damp canvas draping my shoulders I exhibited the Nonconformist conscience of the 'eighties at its best.

Aunt Margaret was always unexpectedly manageable on the subject of "The Wakes", this being due, I think, to her supposition that "The Wakes" was nothing but wedges of ice-cream, corkscrews of ginger-bread and circular horses. This was true of the outskirts of "The Wakes", but not so true of deeper in, and it was as a pensioner of Aunt Margaret, who would not have gone to see Irving even in London, and to whom the local music-hall was hardly distinguishable from the local mortuary, that I saw something of life at "The Wakes". By a judicious outlay of one of her shillings, I have been admitted into the presence and have shaken hands with a lady who had just turned the scale at thirty stones; I have been one of an attentive semicircle while another public character – on the thin side this one! – has devoured an Arabian scimitar, a couple of bradawls and a toasting-fork; and I have sat in a front seat – twopence extra! – while a Russian count has, at a range of twenty yards, accurately delimited in carving-knives the figure of a young lady in a Swiss bolero, a short petticoat and Hessian boots with scarlet laces. To this young lady I became, partly because she had yellow hair and partly because her life seemed a hard one, almost morbidly attached, and I had many plans by which, if it could only be managed, she could be transferred from the Russian count to my mother, so that she could live with us. I have turned the matter over in my mind as I have lain in bed while "The Wakes" still flared yellow against the window blind and surged up murmurously against the walls of the quiet house. And all the time I was learning the mind of my elders and betters, as fishermen learn a dangerous coast, by going out to sea – and coming in. There was a father to be reckoned with; and still more to the point, a mother; there was Aunt Margaret, who said "you" when she was speaking to two of us and "thou" when there was only one, partly because she thereby achieved a more perfect truth of intercourse, and partly because it was thus that Moses and the Lord habitually conversed; and there was Uncle William, whose formidable code of morals was unimpaired even by the lassitudes and laxities of living in Bowdon. Not for nothing had I for some thirteen years sailed in and out of such seas. The navigable channel twisted and turned upon itself, so that in the very era in which I had known Sanger's Circus forbidden, I saw Wombwell's Menagerie, which also descended on us processionally, allowed. There were levitical shallows where one's argument, once aground, could not get afloat again; there were rocks which the assault of many waters had washed but never worn away. And there were harbours; seldom since – never on the tamer coasts where I have traded - have I found such sudden harbours, such certitude and safety, such stillness and such depth – such a reflection of the stars.

VIII
THE QUARRY WHENCE —

MANCHESTER was always too near, rather an overpowering contiguity. And Manchester nowadays is nearer still. Every few minutes Manchester stretches forth a tentacle and draws it back again; only a touch, but a reminder. Every few minutes around that corner into the ancient market-place the tramcar occurs, *debonair*, unfatigued. To go into Manchester by road in the old days was to have little to do and a long summer afternoon in which to do it – to be minded rather to travel than arrive. Three horses, the front one exiguously connected with the vehicle behind, achieved the journey, not without signs of acute personal inconvenience at the end. The way in the old days was generally by train, and the train separates even as it joins – the enclosed life of the carriage, the unreality of the country outside, the very necessity of waiting isolated, impotent for the something fifty-nine. Many mental readjustments must have come of that swift unwrapping by the car of the paved and lighted road. I know quite well now that between Ashton-on-the-Hill and Manchester it is all of a familiar piece. In the old days we were an isolated people.

We were more than that. We who lived in Ashton-on-the-Hill lived in the capital of a defined territory. We were metropolitans, and in relation to the communities of Seeke, Benton, Iveley and Duckingtown, unmistakably *the thing*. We bore without self-consciousness the presence in our social system of a Badminton Club. It met in the Armoury on Saturday afternoons, a very exclusive assemblage, admission to which was by rules always acted on but not precisely defined, though it was just as well for candidates to communicate with the Established Church. I have, at any rate, seen the members walking home through the crowd "after Badminton", talking unconcernedly among themselves, airing the deportment which may be supposed to come of that highly-mannered game, but hardly noticed, even so, in the varied panorama exhibited by our main street on Saturday night. The London Missionary Society, again, knew the facts about us. We were the headquarters of an "auxiliary"; a glance down that table of annual collections displayed once again in a striking manner who in our territories was who. I remember a family which began a chapter of brilliant social success by removing from Duckingtown to Ashton-on-the-Hill. It is true that later they left us for one of the Cheshire suburbs of Manchester. The same thing has happened to Ashton-on-the-Hill since then - will happen again. After all, there is in society as in sainthood the stage higher, and we had them when they were in their ascendant, if not at their meridian.

And so it was that people paid Ashton-on-the-Hill the compliment of "driving into it", and often in the quiet afternoon I have seen in our main street the equipages of a widespread aristocracy, the carriages of people who lived in square stone houses in the smooth enfoldings of the hills beyond Stallbridge. Almost any afternoon one might see the carriage of a certain cotton lord from Iveley, the mantle and bonnet-strings and the successive chins of the cotton lord's wife discernible through the bevelled glass – an imposing terracement of chins. She also had "driven in". She had probably announced at dinner – which being dinner in fact was still dinner in name – that she would "drive into Ashton-on-the-Hill this afternoon". She had driven in to Walmsley's, and in nothing did the town show its metropolitan character so well as in the possession of the ancient and stately emporium of drapery known to us and to all our provinces as Walmsley's. It was a shop of deep recesses, low in the roof and incurably impregnated with an odour of aprons and alpaca. It was one of the surprises of a shop rich in architectural unexpectedness that by entering at one door and walking between the two counters whithersoever the aisle might lead, one came out by another door opening on to the same street. This was because the business had added one shop unto another, and at the spot within, exactly where the frontier wall had been, there was a sort of Moslem pulpit reached by an adventurous flight of steps, and in this alcove Mr. Walmsley himself, when not walking in his shop much as Napoleon walked the deck, or superintending on summer mornings the watering of the floor out of a garden can, could be seen intent on the larger accountancy. No town ever numbered in its citizenship a statelier tradesman or one more perfectly matured in that settled order of things wherein bills mature into "accounts rendered" and are finally paid, equally without fluster and without fail; nor had cotton lordship or the wifehood of cotton lordship many incidentals more agreeable than to be conducted across the pavement to the carriage, to be shut in and bowed away by that senatorial presence with the iron-grey hair, and the two deep lines whereby the corners of the mouth were related on either side to the heavy elaborate nose. The shop now belongs to the Government. I perceive without enthusiasm that it houses a new-fangled Government department of which every town in the country has the exact depressing duplicate. Of such are the levellings and the obliterations of the times!

In other respects also the town begins to wear the common face of the age. Twice a night the evacuation of the picture-houses disturbs the organic life of the town. There are music-halls, terra-cotta repetitions of the common pattern, conduit pipes from the central fount of variety art, and turned on here, as elsewhere, every night at seven and something to nine. It is no shame in anyone to resort thereto, but in those old days such was the niceness of our nose for these things, there was an ethical distinction between the theatre at our own doors to which we did not go and the one in Manchester, to which we travelled by the 6.19; and as for the music-hall, it was rather emphatically a place which we had not been inside. Only askance did one know the street in which its mysteries proceeded.

But I know the haunts in which the old spirit of the place still dwells. The side streets remain the side streets of the factory town. Every door upon the street reveals a section of the same interior, the same chest of drawers facing the fireplace, and on it the same wax flowers under the same glass dome, the piano with its wool mats – the head of Dickens at the fanlight staring life back in the face. Some casual gossip simmers up in the street. An elderly woman of considerable and fully admitted amplitude crosses over in a striped petticoat, carrying a cup in her hand. The loan effected, she stays and involves herself in an argument in which her sum of years gives her an authority - " 'E were a young felly when our 'Annah Mary were born". A young woman seated on the chair between the door and the chest of drawers holds a baby on a very steep and slanting knee, listening to the argument as it goes this way and that. The conversation languishes, and the neighbour from over the way finds, after several times of suspecting so, that "she mun be gooing". A retriever dog opens the door of the corner shop with his nose and disappears, and the street is without any animate life at all. But the machinery in the mill at the back of the houses is a palpable presence in the quietude. The complaint of the machinery is broken at intervals by a faint metallic cry, some mechanical loose jointedness, and at intervals by the sigh of the exhaust pipe. The same quietude walks the main streets. There is something exclusive, private, almost monastic in the quality of the afternoon. It is on Saturday night that Ashton-on-the-Hill still reveals itself a capital – lighting the skies of a benighted hinterland.

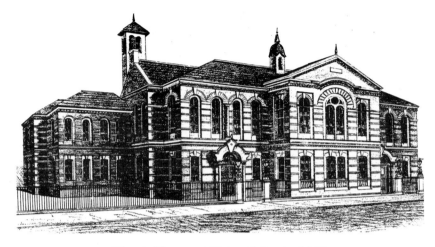

Fig. 6. The new Albion Schools, 1862
(from W. Glover, *History of Ashton-under-Lyne*, p. 265)

Fig. 7. Christmas Dinner at Albion Schoolroom, 1862
(*Illustrated London News*, January 1863)

IX
THE ANNUAL TEA-PARTY

IT was the morning of Christmas Day. The school rose high out of a huddle of small houses in narrow streets, and the snow on the lower roofs around, thawed and frozen again till it would have cut like a cake, reflected a shrill thin light. The bare windows of the Young Men's First Class Room looked out over these upper spaces, and every detail of the Young Men's First Class Room was exposed to the scrutiny of the morning - the photographs of former school "superintendents", the scenes from the Life of David on black rollers, the leaning towers of shiny Bibles, Miss Cheeseman's complexion, Miss Cheeseman's apron, which, though plain, was generously cut and of a high gloss, the plate of bread and butter which Miss Cheeseman carried in her hands. The room though hard and shiny was not cold. A fire of institutional immensity burned at one end behind the fencing of a high fireguard, and around the fireguard stood a congress of corpulent tea-urns, tea-urns with black spouts and mountings, which were kept, except at Christmas, in the basement of the schools, probably with the blue silk Whitsuntide banner, and probably not – only the schoolkeeper knew. The schoolkeeper, in most of his Sunday clothes, was busy in the large room next door. With the assistance of his wife and his eldest son, he was erecting tables at regular spaces down the floor. Even as he worked, the nakedness of the tables began to clothe itself in white apparel; wooden forms were dragged shrieking over the floor, and at the end of each table a flock of white tea-cups clamoured the news of their arrival. As the order of the day became more precise, the tea-cups telescoped into one another, and curled snake-like in the saucers which were heaped several decks high and by now the room had lost its slightly penitential character. It was unmistakable that the Christmas tea-party was about to be held. People who had been at former tea-parties knew that when the gases were lighted and certain exhalations were mounting from the table, the room would become intimate, exclusive, esoteric – definitely "an interior". The profuse steaming of the window-panes was always an indication that the congregation was welded into one entity.

It was in preparation for the Christmas tea-party that in the Young Men's First Class Room they were "cutting up". I cannot but think that this process of "cutting up" had got rather into the hands of a clique. It consisted merely in the reduction of loaves and tea-cakes and pounds of butter – heroic pounds of butter sprawling in soup plates – into the finished article of tea-parties – and yet

37

a ritual with its appointed day and above all its priestesses! To be "asked to go and cut up" was to have an acknowledgment of some standing in the congregation; it was an admission into a subsection of the elect, and it slightly altered one's attitude to the tea-party, turning one's participation in the affair into an act of some self-sacrifice. There were other people to whom the tea-party was genuinely a treat. They sat passive, receptive, taking their fill. On the whole the tea-party was one of those functions in which it was socially preferable to stand and wait, to maintain one's reservations. At the entertainment which followed, those who had "cut up" and turned the taps of the urns became definitely aloof, gregarious together at the back of the room. Composed and intimate talk of the Wright's dance, an approaching affair of some splendour, for which all the town cabs had been engaged, was general among them; the use of Christian names was a habit. The atmosphere around them was indeed bathed in the warm perfume of their common intimacies, and Gladys, leaning forward, would say something allusive, something cryptic, which was infallibly understood by Gertrude, four places from her along the form. They were unmistakeably "a set".

By an arrangement which had been born out of the fitness of things, and for which no ratification could be found in any minute of the congregation, the "cutting up" was under the direction of Miss Cheeseman. Miss Cheeseman moved with much certitude and composure in the affairs both of this world and the next, dealing with the Ultimate First Cause much as she dealt with the senior deacon – confidentially and on the footing of what was exactly due from her to Him, from Him to her. A cordial and not unserviceable co-operation with His designs on the world was the exact quality of her attitude, and the class which she taught Sunday by Sunday – one of the senior classes for girls – was accounted the most efficient in the school. Its organization was indeed so high that it had its own picnic every summer to the Corporation Water works, an engagement which had to accommodate itself with Miss Cheeseman's annual visit to Eastbourne. Her recurring visits to Eastbourne, where she was known to have friends, were an impressive proof of her social consequence. She allowed it to be known vaguely that her savoir-faire was equal even to the difficult exactions of the South Coast. This morning she moved about the room a serene mature presence, making bread and butter herself, surveying the bread and butter made by other people. One or two young men of the congregation dropped in to cast a masculine eye on the preparations. There was some talk of a disturbed night; it was generally agreed that the music of the "waits" had been despicable and at every house represented in the company the postman had been late. The presence of the men caused some falling off in the assiduity of the preparations. Mr. Morris, a rising office-bearer with very modern views on church-music, begged from Miss Cheeseman a piece of crust. She spread it for him with butter, and he sat on the table swinging his legs. The conversation became general, and then, though a noticeable amount remained to be done, several of the girls took off their aprons and began putting on their gloves, discovering that they must go. The schoolkeeper's wife finished it off.

Meanwhile, in yet another apartment of the school the choir was ridden by the preoccupations of those who practise in public a difficult art. Christmas Day was no carnival with our choir. On Christmas morning they had their last rehearsal, drifting in twos and threes to the place of practice with Novello editions under their arms. There are pitfalls in the "Messiah" of which the most nimble contrapuntalist is not sure till he is safely past them. There is that penultimate Hallelujah, the one before the clincher, the one that hangs poised on the abyss – that abyss which tingles with the possibility of a sensational and solitary disaster. On Christmas morning the choir could be heard achieving the ultimate polish – "Wonderful! Counsellor! the Mighty God! the Everlasting Father! the Prince of Peace!" It broke sharp and sudden as artillery fire over the deserted street, where only a stray milk-cart crunched the quiet snow; and to this day I cannot hear the opening bars of "Comfort ye" but there breaks in upon the suavity and certitude of the melody the tinkle through a distant door of tea-cups as the schoolkeeper's wife and two odd women began to get forward with the washing-up. I also see the steam on the school windows beginning to be profuse.

X
REMEMBER THAT THOU KEEP HOLY —

AMONG the Ten Commandments, this one relating to Sunday had the distinction of being enacted personally against me. I had not known sin but by this law! It had other distinctions. It had, for example, the curious character of being the one on which my elders and betters insisted the most, and yet the only one to which they could be caught admitting large and flagrant exceptions. The working principle seemed to be the offering of burnt sacrifices - some of us must be told off to profane the Sabbath in order that others might keep it the more holy. There were, for example, the coachman and footman of Mr. Henry Stonor, who spent a lot of his life in and out of Parliament and had another house in London which few of us had seen. It was a curious fact that while Mr. Stonor's house in Ashton-on-the-Hill was a "Hall", his other house in Onslow Gardens had a number, and I was once told that when his duties in Parliament were over for the day, he went home in a cab or – more inexplicably still – in a train which ran underground. The pondering which I did over this fact did more than anything else I can remember to enlighten my youth as to the majesty of distant London. For in Ashton-on-the-Hill, Mr. Stonor always drove. I shall never think of him as doing anything else except driving – or presiding. At any rate, it always took two men – a coachman and a footman – to convey him to Chapel and there were not only his coachman and footman but the serving men of all the other aristocracy whose carriages on Sunday morning raised Wycliffe Street – where Wycliffe Chapel was – into relationship with the purlieus of the Free Trade Hall on a Hallé night – the same carriages were indeed to be seen on both expeditions. Now from their fur capes in winter and their slashed waistcoats in summer, their long upper lips and frozen faces, to say nothing of the cockades in their hats and their remarkable habit of folding their arms beneath their chins, these men on the box of Mr. Stonor's carriage were palpably Mr. Stonor's men – servants and menservants were specifically named by their name and calling in the authoritative text. "Thou nor thy son, nor thy daughter, thy manservant nor thy maid-servant". The commandment could hardly have spoken plainer! A wrong-headed person might even have argued that allowing for change of fashion in the traction of vehicles, Mr. Stonor's carriage horses came unquestionably under the general descriptive category of "cattle", which again were to do no manner of work. I have actually known people to glance after Mr. Stonor's carriage in the street and speak of his horses appraisingly as "cattle". In taking Mr. Stonor to his devotions in the back pew at Wycliffe Chapel twice every Sunday (when Parliament was "up") – four journeys, there and back, Mr. Stonor's horses had on the whole a busy day, and yet on this very question of Sunday observance Mr. Stonor was what one might call a stickler; on no other question more so. The only thing he would allow to be driven through the commandment relating to Sunday was a coach and two.

It was like this all through. The law twisted and winded and turned back upon itself; there were deeps that looked shallow and shallows that looked deep, and yet no one among us ever missed the channel of correct Sunday conduct, or if he did, he missed it on purpose. I could not to this day define a breach of the Sabbath, but I should always know one when I saw it. For example! The *Manchester Guardian* – a not wholly unspiritual organ – was put carefully into a kitchen drawer on Saturday night and in the length and breadth of Sunday never dared to show its face, but the *Christian World*, which gave on the whole a comprehensive review of the secular world, was allowed out all day and cast a noticeable shade over the tea-table. Knitting – sober and godly occupation – was for some reason almost vindictively banned, but cooking was to some extent encouraged. Not so much as a yard of clothes-line was suffered on the drying-ground and clothes-pegs were swept away on Saturday night like unclean things. There had been, rather before my time, a tremendous battle on the general question of fiction. Fiction at any time! I had elderly aunts who could not even in my day say the word "novel" without a slight darkening of the voice, any more than they could say "cards". But the first battle having been decided in favour of fiction, another one had been fought on the further question of fiction on Sunday. George Eliot came to be allowed. She treated of a life which was recognizably like ours and treated of it with much anxiety and sombreness. On the other hand, there was some doubt about Sir Walter Scott. For years he went about the world chiefly in a paper-back edition decorated with an illustration, often highly coloured, sometimes melodramatic. I remember the one which bore a view of Amy Robsart lying dead at the foot of a flight of stairs. It did Sir Walter Scott no good in certain circles! But all these differences between what could be done and what couldn't, were felt to be grounded safely in some true distinction of principle. I think the truth is that they were. Even the sophist whom I have imagined sharpening his logic on Mr. Stonor's horses and Mr. Stonor's men, would have known in his heart that had Mr. Stonor arrived at Wycliffe Chapel in a dog-cart, driven by himself, the spiritual and moral change as between four wheels and two would have been unmistakable and decisive. I doubt if the sophist would have liked to see such a thing done by Mr. Stonor.

There were questions, again, like that of the milk. I never heard it once disputed that the milk must come as usual on Sunday morning. After all the sun rose, and even Aunt Mary, who was a great expert in Sabbath observance and had gone the length of roping off some portion of Saturday night as a "preparation for the next day" – I have heard her say that the shout of brass and fumes of naphtha that went up from the market-place on Saturday night were "no preparation for the next day" – even Aunt Mary expected her tea and expected it rather urgently on Sunday afternoon, and would have been about the last person in the world to take it in the Russian fashion, without milk. And that being so, Mr. Tame who was our milkman figured quite definitely as a burnt offering in the ritual of the day and was almost totally excluded, though without visible damage to his conduct and character, from the ministration of the Word. Many a time when his cart has made a distant but joyful noise down the street in which Wycliffe Chapel was situated, I have gone after his genial and companionable spirit on his round, and have envied him such freedom among sparrows and sunshine and such unfamiliar glimpses of the empty streets. Having this freedom of Sunday, Mr. Tame must have been familiar with the light that never was on sea or land; must have seen things and aspects of things which no one else had ever seen, except perhaps those who had had to go out of chapel unwell and had no mind to enjoy them. Certainly he was almost the only person who had ever seen our back garden and the passage to our back door at eleven o'clock on Sunday morning. Sometimes when I have been in bed threatening scarlatina I have heard the nails of his shoes, his voice and the ring of his cans wash up against the side door and into the quiet house, just as a flat sea sometimes surges suddenly among the rocks.

And indeed in this matter of Sabbath observance I was always conscious that around and about us there were continents and tracts of earth where the game was simply not played at all. There was always a secular draught blowing through the railway station. I did not myself use the railway station on Sunday for departure or arrival, but several times I have been there to meet those who came on evangelical affairs and, while waiting, I have observed the measured pacing and inhaled the cigars of those who did not excessively fear the Lord. Once in the 2.12 train I saw, curled up in a first-class carriage like a large sleek cat, a famous *prima donna* reading a paper which looked not unlike the *British Weekly* but was really *The Referee*. The 2.12 to Manchester on Sunday was one of those trains which arrived illustrious and temperamental with prolonged travel; the kind of train one "joins" as distinguished from the kind one "takes". I think it must have been setting out from Leeds just about the time when Mr. Harkness was informing us that we should find his text in the Epistle of St. Paul to the Ephesians, and its oncoming and perseverance must have overlapped all that had happened to us since then, including Sunday's dinner. An impressive fact! And when it stopped at Ashton-on-the-Hill chiefly for the collection of tickets, its carriages were seats of old settlements and were littered with the ruin and *ennui* of men's lives – with packs of cards and dismembered Sunday papers, and bottles and cups and saucers and little dogs. From the accident that the 2.12 arrived at almost the identical moment appointed for the opening of Sunday School, there must be very many who never saw it and may think that I overstate the excitement of its haughty and insolent agnosticism. But that is not so. It seldom arrived without having collected from numerous sidings in the West Riding, rich accretions of theatrical and Bohemian interest. I have watched while comedians with ripe, not to say over-ripe, faces have visited hatless ladies several compartments away and have addressed them through the carriage window in a tone of voice which left no room for doubt that they knew them quite well. I have heard them say in response to languid inquiry that they did not know what Ashton-on-the-Hill was – "some stopping place". And so indeed it was – to me, but not to them!

There was one Sunday when I saw the opera company which was to play that week at our own theatre actually descend upon us. I followed them out of the station into the street, where the sun was causing a remarkable eruption of tar between the tram-lines and glinting powerfully on the silk hat and shiny hymn-book of a town missionary whose disappearance down a side street was momentarily almost the only sign of life in the deep Sunday swoon of the town. In the porch of the Methodist New Connexion Chapel two young men in lavender trousers and longish frockcoats could be seen withdrawn into the shade, indicating some executive relationship with the faint treble hymn which could be heard going on inside. Every shop window had gone behind its blue or yellow blind, and the blind of Miss Waterhouse, the confectioner, having descended imperfectly, the segment of a cut-glass vessel containing crumbs and flies was exposed to view and was destined to remain exposed all Sunday. But for this, the street was featureless, except that from the show-case of Mr. Mottershead, the dentist, several upper and lower rows and one example of both rows complete, smiled into the blank prospect with a brilliant urbanity. A lofty bell which had been ringing rapidly and inexplicably in the church tower suddenly stopped. And Sunday took the operatic company and swallowed it up. From the station door the whole group of them put out into it like horses putting out into a lake, and then they sank below the surface and the stagnation of the town closed over their heads, nor was there anything to show a few minutes later that they had even arrived, except that a spring cart rattled through the street with basket luggage and that in Modena Street, where such people lived, there arose a faint exhalation of steak and onions. And the spectacle being exhausted, I ran home past the blue and yellow window blinds with only my own reflection for company, for I had already been out quite long enough on Sunday seeing off a train.

XI
THE FIRST VIOLIN

IT had once been a chapel. So much was clear from its oblong configuration – a building in which it had been more important to hear than to see, with two shallow galleries and a deep one facing the stage. And as they were still using up quantities of maroon brocade with tassels, I judged it to have been a Dissenting chapel, belonging to one of the more recondite sects, small in number and very dainty of belief, for maroon hangings are the mark of the higher Nonconformity, just as white lawn is the mark of the Church of England and purple velvet that of Rome. When and at what conjecture in the rise and fall of faiths it became a music-hall I hardly know, but if one came early, when the audience was still arriving in ones and twos, it might still have been a chapel, and the tilting of the plush seats punctuated one's reverie very much like the desultory opening and shutting of pew doors – the same note of preparation for a quiet, customary event. But here the illusion ceased, for instead of the pulpit with its plush and morocco, the *carafe* of water with the down-turned glass, and the demure glimmer of light through an egg-shell globe, there was a drop-curtain, and on the drop-curtain a highly seductive view of life on the North Coast of Africa, with the god Pan playing some part.

For my part I never thought he had enough elbow-room for a mannered instrument like the violin. The brass rail which cut off the orchestra from the stalls irked him, and his hand used to beat softly against the curtain when he was hard at work on his top string. Once when I was on the front row of the stalls he even smote me on the knee with his knuckle. The assault occurred in the fluent passage of "Raymond", and he opened his pale-blue eyes and glanced at me along the slope of the instrument, hoping that I should understand. And then when he was on his low string he had to allow for the neck of the other "first", a pathetic figure so placed as to have no view whatever of the stage, though when the house was convulsed he would pop up and peer over the stage, still sawing. And yet the First Violin was not without learning in the technique of his art, and particularly was he skilled in the reading of obscure and not infrequently corrupt musical text. Much journeying to and fro in the jungle of song and badinage and dance had given him fortitude for the doubling back of the path and a kind of instinct for the right way through. And this, though the finger-posts were laconic and far between! Several sheets of blank music-paper and then in the middle of a page in a spiky hand the words "Father Brings the

Milk Home in the Morning" and two thumb-marks! The treble of the refrain pushes on with sudden volubility for several bars, and then a long passage has been scored out by someone who seems to have been in a temper, and the thread is resumed over the next page but one, and is pursued through a good deal of ambiguity and some sticking-plaster, until suddenly out of the mist there shoots an alarming rocket of semi-quavers. The chorus is repeated as often as it suffices Miss Wax Vesta to change for the next song. The First Violin has got to know it – he lets it go. And Miss Vesta having signalled that she is ready, the conductor taps twice and stops matters on a chord which is still unresolved. The First Violin makes no protest. He turns over his manuscript. "I'm a Dashing Militaire", remarks the spiky hand, and Miss Vesta herself appears – a very final corroboration of the announcement. She walks several times the breadth of the stage to induce that rapport between herself and the audience which is a condition of her art. Incidentally she hums the melody hard through her teeth, bringing the orchestra by the scruff of its neck into the rhythm. The First Violin glances from her to his music and back to her again, anxious to be taught. By and by he has it right. His violin is frosty with resin-dust for a considerable area around the bridge.

But I admire him most at those moments when the orchestra, having made a false start, gathers round and becomes a parliament of clashing and conflicting views; when the voice of an unseen presence at the wings is hissing "No, no, the Spring Song"; when the dancer on whom the curtain has just risen is held up against a black-velvet background in an effective preliminary attitude of some constraint which in the anatomical nature of things she cannot preserve much longer. The conductor is receiving suggestions from right and left, from the cornet player who has removed his instrument an inch from his mouth to enforce a theory which he holds rather strongly – from everybody except the broad-backed man at the piano, who sits deep down and in some detachment, and to whom, however they settle it, it is sure to resolve itself into "pom" with the left and "pom-pom" with the right. I suspect the First Violin on such occasions of a tendency to giggle; certainly there is in his eye a cheerful recognition of the fact that in art as in life the ideal is always some way ahead. He glances to this effect at the derisive audience over his brass rail, and when eventually they find the right place and the voice at the wings is appeased and the lady on the stage released, he goes on as though nothing worth mentioning had occurred – a happy warrior!

* * *

Two ducks shouldered through the ornamental water, sitting deep, saying something fretful. They left four oblique curling rollers behind them as they swam. On this Sunday morning they were the only entertainment in the recreation ground, for a third duck in deep apathy on a stony island was not spectacular. The smoke from a row of new houses over the palings beat down over the geometrical flowerbeds, and on everything beneath a grey, racing sky there was an unevaporated ooze – on the metal battledores which warned one off the grass, on all the cast-iron in which the recreation ground is rich, on the swings which stood like the gallows in an asphalt annexe. Down the path, the centre of a fidgety family group, came the First Violin. His right hand was on the brass rail of a perambulator; in his other hand there was a newspaper with a slab of reading matter turned up. But the reading went slowly, for the youngest but one, who was coming to years of indiscretion, exhibited a stubborn preference for walking over the benches along the path, a mode of progression which involved a good deal of quarrelling with his kindred and some risk. The First Violin intervened in the dispute at regular intervals. Once he was busy for some time extracting damp gravel from the knees and palms of the youngest but one. And none of those who looked on but I, knew that he led a band, sat night by night in the draught which comes from the little door under the stage, the draught which is nectarously flavoured with an escape of gas; that he co-operated in public with the accepted wits – that ladies who were "the rage" dragged him by the scruff of his neck into the rhythm of a song. Slowly the family group worked its way home – twice round the ornamental water and into the road, the perambulator agitated violently on the stones. Progress was hampered all the way home by the inability of the youngest but two to be satisfied until he had touched with his five fingers each separate garden railing they passed. More than once the First Violin turned and called him on, urging the nearness of dinner-time. And then he was gathered into the empty distances of rather a long street. It was off hours with the First Violin.

XII
THE SERMONS

WE used to call it alternatively "The Anniversary" or "The Sermons". Our elders, who were nearer to the tradition than we were, dropped the definite article completely and spoke of "Sermons", just as though it had been a word like Epiphany. It was, for example, very meet and proper to get the house nice and clean "before Sermons". I have frequently heard "The Sermons", used as an annual event for the determination of all contiguous dates. Used thus, I have known it to figure not seldom as the last word in an argument. Aunt Mary, who never knew when she was beaten about a date, would often stun her opponent with "The Sermons". As thus. "Whatever you may say, they were married in April. I ought to know because I know I had my Sermons bonnet on. It was a brown chip with white roses. I hadn't had it out of the box more than twice and mother said" – plainly a clincher!

Being Dissenters and belonging indeed, as one of our best pulpit orators often reminded us, to the dissidence of Dissent, we were but vaguely conscious of Lent. It began about the time we were eating pancakes, but ran the full length of its course underground and did not come to the surface again until Good Friday, the day on which we hoped to take our first picnic to the Corporation Waterworks. It had been decided by someone long before us – rather too hastily, I think – that the giving up of sugar in Lent or the getting up at six-thirty in Lent when seven would have done, not only failed to impress the Lord but that it actually vexed Him. To make a point of things like this was to draw a red herring across that ruthless pursuit of scheduled sin in which we figured the Lord as incessantly engaged. At any rate, we did not keep Lent, and there was not one of us could have told whether the long procession of the Sundays after Trinity was going on or had come to an end.

But in the highway of our ecclesiastical year – otherwise all of a piece – the Anniversary was a stopping-place where the waters gushed forth. On this day the annual sermons were preached by someone eminent – two sermons with an address in the afternoon to the children thrown in – and the annual collections taken on behalf of the Sunday Schools. Such was the event defined in terms of its own skeleton and so it figured on the black notice-board by the chapel door. But this was not how it figured in our minds. Like the expectation of an important guest, it was always the cause of a domestic stampede. Houses were represented in the congregation in which – such was the pressure of life – no

48

Sunday dinner was cooked on this day, and others, only a degree less absorbed, in which the joint was cooked on Saturday night and cut into cold and without potatoes on Sunday. Wycliffe Chapel itself worked all day like a furnace, receiving through its doors immense congregations and transforming them into apostolic steam of the very highest pressure. On all other Sundays in the year, every man's pew in Wycliffe Chapel was his castle, defended by a door which closed with a snap and could be latched. Once upon a time a tall blonde woman, who was to sing in opera the next week at the local theatre, came to Wycliffe Chapel, having heard, as it afterwards leaked out, that the music was good. Wandering up and down the aisle, she looked like someone who had arrived in Blackpool without first engaging apartments. At last some one let her in to a pew and she disappeared from a situation the publicity of which must have been painful even to an opera singer. But on Sermons Sunday the regular pew-holders were swamped, and wanted to be. In the evening it was no uncommon thing for forms to be brought into the aisles to accommodate the invasion of those who were not of our fold. Did I say it was no uncommon thing? It was in point of fact a regular thing. I never knew it not to happen, and it is certain that the Anniversary would have been a failure and the eminent preacher would have had to be judged not worth his salt, if in the evening they had not had to bring forms into the aisles. The removal of these forms so that the population in the pews might be able to emerge, was an impressive accompaniment to the last hymn. The profuse streaming of the frosted windows and a slight perspiration noticeable on the pale-blue organ pipes was another indication that the right congregational spirit had been achieved.

With Mr. Ogden Green, Sermons Sunday was a day of early and late. Mr. Ogden Green was the proprietor of a very highly esteemed fancy-shop in which his wife and his wife's sister held quiet communion with customers all the day, chiefly on crewel work. There were February afternoons in Ashton-on-the-Hill when the main street presented nothing to the eye except the Manchester tram-car anchored in sloth and stagnation and a clerk with a ruler in his mouth toiling behind the wire blind of the solicitor's office, but it would not be long before the aprons and petticoats slung across a brass rail in the window of Mrs. Ogden Green's shop would be parted and ten chilly fingers would come on view matching wool in the faint blue light. Mr. Ogden Green, though the head of this establishment and of the tailor's shop next door, and available for the settlement of the larger questions which arose in the day's trade, gave himself chiefly to duties connected with the Congregational Chapel and the Liberal Party. Through both his shops there blew a continual breeze of the public spirit. He was a man who possessed in a very striking degree the committee mind. His life was almost a permanent committee meeting. His correspondence was largely on printed post-cards, his appointments chiefly at half-past seven o'clock at night in vestries and class-rooms furtively lighted with single gas jets which had developed prongs. Through constant attendance at committee meetings there had crept into his English style a marked infusion of Latinity. There were moments in which he expressed himself in pure Latin, for the paper which he had placed on the chairman's table before the meeting began contained the *agenda*. Whether he knew that the *agenda* were "the things meet to be done" is, I think, open to some doubt, for his Latin was rather practical and administrative than scholastic, but it is quite certain that if a committee rose without fixing any time for its re-assembly, he knew as with a flash, that it had adjourned *sine die,* and the committee itself might have been neither a "general" nor an "executive" but a committee *ad hoc*, which was a committee elected to get the best terms out of the railway company for the Whitsuntide excursion, and nothing else. And it was in his shop and even at his shop door that questions which would come up at those committee meetings were cut and dried – it was a frequent complaint of Mr. Ogden Green's opponents at meetings of committees that they had come finding "everything cut and dried", a favourite stroke of irony indicating that the meeting need not have been held at all and that Mr. Ogden Green might just as well settle for and by himself whether the refreshments were to take the form of "a plain tea" or a "knife and fork tea".

"The Anniversary" or "The Sermons" may well, as we can see, have been his very busy day. He did everything for "The Sermons" except listen to them. The truth was that the variety and extent of his administrative duties excused him over many years from all the arduous moments which occur in church attendance. He was in the choir, and there was rarely a service in which Mr. Tom Brown, who sang bass next to him and with whom he ran neck to neck in those winding and tortuous passages for the basses which are such a plague in oratorio, had not to raise his knees almost to his chin in order to let Mr. Ogden Green pass out – and afterwards pass in – on some matter which had occurred to him. I do not know that for many years he ever really heard any sermon all through, for if he was not in the chapel-porch or even in the street, he was in the vestry busy among collection boxes or he was inspecting the heating apparatus, and often when a difficult text had been given out and the conclusion of the whole matter was not even within sight, his face, framed in a stiff beard which had once been sandy and was now grey, could be seen outside passing the side windows of the chapel and enviably dappled by the sun of Sunday morning, like unto which there is no sun.

Every year the Sermons were preached by one of the celebrities of our schism: it might be Dale of Birmingham, or Berry of Wolverhampton, or Bruce of Huddersfield, but it was Paul certainly "somebody of somewhere" like who was "of Tarsus". And yet the supreme interest of the day was not exposition but finance. What would the collections "realize". The answer to this question was given out at night just after the last hymn and before we broke away. Every head was arrested at a sort of half-way stopping-place to the devotional attitude. We bent our shoulders to receive the blessing, but lifted our heads to hear the news. The organist above the pulpit left his stops out and turned round on the organ seat to hear what it would be, and the contraltos and sopranos could be seen peering over the gallery ledge – but then the contraltos and sopranos enjoyed the status of performers and it was obvious that less was expected of them in point of reverence than of me. The collecting power of our chapel was sensational and in a remote vestry, pitted against the number of verses in "Onward, Christian Soldiers", the counters were counting furiously. Stories got about afterwards of additional gifts made dramatically at the last moment in a passionately desired roundness of figures. In the end it was Mr. Ogden Green who carried the final figures up the pulpit stairs, and he who pulled pulpit eminence by its coat sleeve and passed him the neat addition sum. "I am desired to announce that as a result of today's services the collections have realized the magnificent sum of – and now may the blessing, etc., etc".

Later, supping at our house and concluding a perfect day with coffee and apple-pie, Mr. Ogden Green would lift the curtain of church finance an inch or two, naming the number of five-pound notes in the boxes – several in the morning though they were rare at night – and pinning each one with complete certitude to the coat of its anonymous donor. He spoke with the authority of one who was known to have performed the supremely delicate task of paying the preacher of the day his fee. Like Sir Robert Walpole, he knew – though without cynicism – that every man had his price and what his price was. He had an intimate anecdote in this connection about the Olympian Dr. —.

XIII
THE SUPERIOR QUALITY OF KHAKI

ASHTON-ON-THE-HILL was a barrack town – a famous one. The worst of it is that in circles which I cannot now deem negligible it was known as nothing else than a barrack town. There were men on the North-West Frontier, men swaggering two and two by evening in the *ennui* of the bazaar, and looking over the blistering walls of heated coaling-stations – men on the march and, as we were to learn afterwards from Mr. Kipling, men at Mandalay, who had been collected, stored and dispatched at Ashton-on-the-Hill. We did not know it, or if we did know it we knew it only in our minds, which is hardly knowing a thing at all – not in our consciousness. And so it is that when I think of the land in which we dwelled, how heavy with the odours of sanctity, how girt about by towering crags of sheer character, it seems strange that to all quartermasters and to the General Staff – far away at Simla and hardly less far away at Aldershot – it was merely the place where the Granchesters came from. I think of the Rev. Dr. Conway toasting his delicate shins at Aunt Margaret's parlour fire while he discoursed of "the cause at Ashton-on-the-Hill", to which indeed he had given a lifetime of statesmanship, and it seems strange that it was not for him nor for "the cause" nor yet for our implacable feud between Liberal and Tory, which swayed now this way and now that, and often went the length of sticks and stones, nor even for philharmonics and oratorio, nor yet our homeric collecting for the London Missionary Society that we were known abroad, but because we were the watershed where were collected the Granchesters.

I say that we did not know this, and yet the Mossborough Road along which the barracks were to be sought was always splashed more or less scarlet with their excursions and alarms, their comings in and goings out. Sergeants passed along it with crimson sashes and smaller smalls to their backs than was usual in the general cut of man. They carried blue envelopes up and down to the Post Office – like income-tax envelopes but larger – and privates in Scotch caps with scarlet buttons dusted their trousers with inexpensive canes, and were to be seen at night – if one was along the Mossborough Road at night – entranced by their beloveds. And at odd times of the day which did not seem to correspond with our simple rubric of breakfast and dinner and tea, the bugle-call wandered like a little homeless elf in the green enfoldments of the hills. For the barracks were far away from the familiar prosaic latitudes of the town. They lay out on our questionable frontiers, down at the edge of low tide, where life beat faint and indistinct, murmuring on shores and shallows which were institutional and not domestic. It was on the same forlorn verge that we kept the workhouse and the waterworks and other institutions which needed segregation and space. We had not domesticated the barracks as we had domesticated the Mechanics' Institute or the Wycliffe Day Schools, the steps of which were excavated by the soles of our feet, or the Town Hall, which reeked of us, even when we were not in it, as an empty cask yet reeks of the wine. The barracks belonged to the Government and not to us.

I do not think that many of us had ever known a soldier. Families in which the eldest son had incontinently embraced a military career were, it is true, not entirely unknown, but when it happened it was a family scandal. The event, when it occurred, was often regarded as a salutary lesson to super-tyrannical parents, and our speculations on the subject turned not upon the possibility of our having nourished a Napoleon in our midst, but on the trouble and expense, the exact degree of mortification and ignominy which would be involved in the process known as "buying him out". It was indeed the boast of the Badminton set that numerous officers had lingered in that proud society, and at Wycliffe we had a regular soldier in the congregation. It is true that he was an old soldier far beyond the age of personal combat. But even so we were very conscious of his presence among us – a shadowy spirit for all his solidity of substance – and when Mr. Harkness, our minister, fabricated a military metaphor, a habit which he had caught from St. Paul, I at any rate used to look round hoping that Sergeant Hamilton was listening. The Army had not then modulated into khaki and the ordinary stuff of flesh and blood. It was intensive, far-fetched, cayenne, operatic, and to me looking back, the barracks seem in the 'eighties to have been the real nonconformity of Ashton-on-the-Hill – more nonconformist even than the Parish Church. The Volunteers, it is true, grew out of the common life. They were bone of our bone and hewed from the same quarry whence we were also digged. It was always evident as they paraded along New Street that they had friends and relations on the kerb. A Volunteer, scratched to the depth of his tunic, was only "our Sam" or "your Fred". They ran so to speak a gauntlet of genial recognition from the kerb. But the Volunteers had not yet been baptized by fire. That also was to come later, and meanwhile we associated them firmly in our minds with Saturday afternoon. *We did not believe that the Volunteers were really warlike, or, if it came to it, would fight.*

The truth is that we had next to no "Kultur". I find it astonishing to reflect even from these times how much we lived by conscience and how little by law - how in the late 'eighties the State had left us high and dry in our own conceits, so that the State had indeed become no more to us than such a romantic trouble of the sea as is always retained by the shell-the thunder mainly of distant eloquence, and the murmurs of an element in which leviathans disported themselves at play. Royalty was still communing with itself in the long widowhood of Balmoral, and was an invisible and almost an impalpable thing, faintly remembered by some of our elders who had seen it in a crinoline. Mr. Chamberlain had not yet discovered the Empire. There was no Labour Party. The unemployed were still "beggars", personages not yet taken up by sociology and still belonging to the rag-bag of romance. And, knowing so little of the central State, we had built little States of our own, thinking to abide in them for ever. It was the day when all Israel lived habitually in tents. I know the sensational fact, though no one else knows it, that if Aunt Margaret had not been a Methodist she would have been a Baptist. She confided it to me one Sunday night when she was kept from chapel - "laid aside" was her own form of words - and I sat with her. And I can remember how she spoke of it as a woman who, though wed long and happy years, may yet speak of the lover whom she sent away, seeing him in the firelight – how she toyed with the subject for a moment and then dismissed it. She also was a dweller in tents. And I think that if Aunt Margaret had been suddenly challenged by the sentry - perhaps when she was challenged - she said "Methodist" - not even "English" and certainly not "Britisher". She lived before the flood. I wonder if *she* knew that Ashton-on-the-Hill was also a barrack town.

XIV
AN OLD TRAM-CAR

IT stood in the further recesses of a back garden, beyond the lawn and the flower-beds and in the hinterland of the rhubarb and other serious vegetation. One part of it was used as a potting-shed, and the shelves and the floor were scattered with crumbs of dusty soil, and there were pyramids of plant pots, and sundry bulbs which had missed their way in life. The other half was a fowl-house giving upon a penitential run. There was an almond-shaped window, on the inside of which a stray feather was lodged. Looking through the window, I found myself peering deep into another intelligence and another eye, the lid of which glided upwards, and then a neck telescoped out and in again, the eye still watching me with suspicion and reserve. The whole structure stood upon four towers of brick. There was something elusively familiar in its contour. I seemed to have seen this building somewhere else, somewhere before, and then I traced a faded lettering. It read "M.C.T.C. Ltd." or some thing of that kind, a fragmentary hieroglyphic, and I realized that this was one of the old cars which used to carry us at something rather faster than a fast walking pace, before posts and wires had cut our streets into bars of music, when the trolley-boy of to-day was still practising on his mother's apron-string – in fact, before the electric car. And I thought of our present cars as one sees them at night, lying out in St. Mary's Gate like liners anchored in the roads, beating up the devious channel into Albert Square, shouldering their way powerfully over loops, their decks level with upper chambers in the village streets of Withington and Fallowfield, and turning the slope of Oxford Road on autumn nights into a chemist's shop of many bottles.

And it surprised me very much that with the eyes of intelligent youth I should have seen this fowl-house and potting-shed hauled through the streets in the wake of others by imperfectly tamed animals who would rather have been excused, and were addicted to unseemly perspiration and to bronchitis; that I might have caught this very one in the morning, perhaps even have missed it, and that I should have been very much in the swim of things on a laborious raft like this. I remember that we who were men about town practised tricks with the old cars, and that they served for accomplishments to which the new cars do not lend themselves, so that these graces are now wiped out of the catalogue of the human arts. It was a great thing in those days to walk out of the car – whilst it was in full career – with one's back square to the horses and one's face set absent-mindedly on the vista of the street, to drop on to a stone-set with one heel, throwing the weight of the body well forward, as the professors used to exhort us, and to do it negligently and casually as though it came by nature. The street was dramatic with the certitude of our alightings. We dropped into Market Street like gulls clawing down on a rocky shore. But the old cars were responsible for one social agony which society does not feel now. The "outsides" in those days sat in two rows back to back, and if they were men of a full habit they sat back against back. And sometimes it would happen that two cars would be brought to a stop side by side, and then the two inside rows on the two cars would find themselves awkwardly *vis-à-vis* in the solitude of midair, with nothing to say. And they would be kept there, not long enough to find conversational openings as the guests do at the long table of a boarding-house *table d'hôte*, but long enough to get their eyes entangled in a mortifying knot. The garden seats were a great innovation, but I do not remember that they became universal in the horse-drawn car. On the garden seat the Britisher can attain to his native isolation. And now the "outsides" ride in glass saloons, and the companies of "outsides" pass one another in the street much as people on the boat returning from the Isle of Man, pass the other people on the boat which is going out.

At the terminus the old car took itself very seriously. Not without such a flourish as befits the end of a chapter successfully reached and rounded off, did its coming end and its going-back begin. With the modern cars, front and back are the same thing. Like the fingers of the tide, they are pushed out to the high-water mark of the suburb. They touch it and are drawn back again into the storehouse of the central life. But in the old days, the car turned bodily round on a pivot somewhere in the centre of its vitals, and this turning was a spectacular thing, a recurring event in the provincial peace of our far confines. At the terminus which I remember best three horses brought the car in, and the leader could only get round on the terms of receiving some latitude on the footpath. On the footpath accordingly he climbed, brushing the parasites from the wall of the public-house, crossing his feet tentatively, the two horses behind him revolving in another circle of a narrower circumference. The driver directed matters from a high office-stool, the guard co-operating conversationally at the leader's mouth, and the nursemaids with the perambulators waiting till there was a running chance. And the horses having wound the car completely on its pivot, always gave it one more wrench, and were generally some distance on another circle before they were brought finally to rest in the straight. The parasites settled against the wall again, and we who were passengers took our places and sat expectantly on maroon plush seats, with our ankles in straw.

One fine summer there was a feminine invasion of the roof, a social innovation in its way. At several tea-tables at which I was present – seen but not heard – the appearance of ladies on the tops of the cars was the subject of comment. Particular instances of a practice which was new were adduced. The names of ladies were mentioned, of ladies who had moral character enough to authorize any new custom, ladies who were emphatically not athletes, and it was reported how this one and that had been seen on the top of a car. And then someone said that "Nobody seemed to think anything of it", and the talk wandered off to something else. It is by such stealthy approaches that the tide of revolution comes in. In England!

XV
ON GOING INTO ETONS

I DO not know who in the household of faith originated the proposal that I should be put into Eton suits or how exactly it came about that, with less support than even Horatio got, I was called on to fight with Ashton-on-the-Hill that prolonged and bitter struggle on the right of an otherwise undistinguished boy to inflict himself upon the eyesight in a jacket that was sensationally too small for him, and added to this the further and graver offence of being the first of its kind that had ever been seen on a live boy in the town. I fought with wild beasts at Ephesus. When the people saw me they rent not my garments, but their own. But I won. I can see now that I was bound to win from the start, if only because those who ordered me into the affair cut off every possible retreat by allowing me only the one kind of jacket and giving my other to the poor. The success of my offensive was due to the fact that it underwent no pause. I was always in season. For some five years it was never possible to tell by looking at me whether it was Saturday or Sunday or Monday. I had that quality which Seneca says is the mark of the perfected character, of being and seeming always the same. The only hope for the myriads of Ashton-onthe-Hill lay in my complete extermination, and even then I should have been still incorrigible, for I should have been seen dead in the thing. I say I do not know who originated the proposal that I should be put into Etons. Probably the idea was conceived by some elder sister or other, on seeing Westminster boys from the top of the 'bus in London at a moment when I was myself at home, up the apple-tree or embedded in the tarpaulin on the roof of the summer-house, but without premonition of what was coming and with no pride in my personal appearance to speak of. To me it was one of several things which I traced as happening, or nearly happening, as the result of having relatives at Altrincham, an ostentatious state of things for which I felt I was not personally to blame, and which led to my being placed every now and then under a microscope and being looked at by several large people who seemed to be quarrelling as to whose turn it was to look next. And then the higher education had recently happened to the family in the person of one of my seniors who had gone to Cambridge. Not without slight but ominous sounds of something splitting, "the 'varsity" was being fitted into a scheme of life which had not been measured for it, and, in the course of the process, life was just one thing after another, one thing being the discovery in the overcoat pocket of the same senior, of a briar pipe in an advanced stage of encrustation, and another, the lifting of an undergraduate voice in guarded praise of the merits of beer. I do not know whether my Etons were a part of this revival of learning which in promoting one of us to the university sent several others back to school, the number including Aunt Margaret, who did not at all want to go and thought that beer and tobacco were only taken by the damned. Certainly they were contemporary with this movement, and Etons are, when one comes to think of it, scholastic things.

And perhaps it would be the easier course to suppose that Eton jackets happened to me just because the proper time had come and there was some momentary doubt what to do with me next. But that would not be true. The fall of a sparrow to the ground is an event which has been brewing through centuries of illustrious history, and to think of my Eton jackets as a bolt from the blue would be to leave out of account all the gathered and gathering electricity which they merely announced. I went forth as a straw indicating a new direction of the wind. The profound and moving truth has to be stated that over large tracts of Wycliffe Chapel we were ceasing to be ourselves. We were losing caste. The long rabbinical winter was breaking up, and the whole settlement was pruning its feathers in every wind that blew. The Surridge family was distraught with new-fangled ideas. One of the Miss Surridges went to Germany, and returned pronouncing Lancashire names like Mendelssohn and Mozart as they are pronounced in Prague, and while Mr. Surridge himself was hollow only as to the chest and cheeks, his sons began almost to disappear in new places at the waist, gave an impression of being only accidentally caught in mufti, and cultivated moustaches which were distinctly visible even to those who followed directly behind them up the aisle. There were some among us who got to know on the occasion of annual visits to Llandudno that the Anglican Prayer Book, so far from being an uncharted sea, contains matter in smaller print which carries one without disaster from crisis to crisis of ritual, and by strict attention to these directions they almost acquired the unconcern of High Anglicans. In Mr. Darlington's family, where they took everything cerebrally, there was a fearful outbreak of Egyptology. Amid these signs and portents I went precipitately into Etons. The bold and unflinching character of the spirit may be measured by the circumstance that while they were preparing me on the altar, it was cynically suggested that the *tout ensemble* would be more complete by the addition of a top-hat, and a top-hat also would have happened to me if it had not been vetoed by the masculine intelligence which, since it finally paid, had in extreme cases the final word. My resemblance to the haughty and patrician youths on Mr. Ogden Green's fashion-plates remained therefore one of ambition and general direction, and was never quite complete. But it was near enough for the unaired streets of Ashton-on-the-Hill. I have known myself on Saturday night to stop important conversations of the Medes and Persians at twenty-five yards' range, and in all errands, whether of my own or of other people, I had to calculate for the liberation of the National Schools at twelve and four as sailors take their bearings at sea. The mistake of a fraction would have made all the difference. I should have been stoned like Stephen.

And yet I often thought, one against so many as I was, that the missiles came from a people which itself lived in a glass house. Far more sensational things happened to Ashton-on-the-Hill in this very matter of clothes than ever happened to me. It was, for example, a community which did not moult. It is of the nature of moulting that a gradual deterioration should be followed by an equally imperceptible process of repair, and that sudden and static perfection should never be attained. But Ashton-onthe-Hill had the personal habit of a butterfly which bursts forth. There was that yearly event of Whit-Sunday. No one but an expert in Lancashire would have known what was coming, nor was there anything to indicate it the night before but a general hurrying to and fro with paper bags which from their pneumatic condition and the circumstance that trimmings protruded at the mouth might be guessed to contain hats. Band-boxes and a few drops of rain were indeed the marks of the Saturday night before Whit-Sunday. Nothing else! And yet the next day the thing occurred with such precision that whereas at noon it had not begun, by a quarter-past two it was accomplished, and Wycliffe Sunday School, a vast parterre of tulips and geraniums, rose to attack the first Whitsuntide hymn on the paper. It was the moment of moments for a worm to turn critic and inquire of the assembled community, in the tone of one who neither expects nor desires an answer, where it got that hat! But I never turned. Alas for the poor spirits of the minority of one!

XVI
THE NORTH SHORE

PRESTON was too soon to look for it. There was indeed a tidal river at Preston, and the river, seen through the lattice of the bridge, carried light masts and vanished to the left in its own silver, wearing that slight look of haste and dedication which tidal rivers often have when they are coming to their fate in the sea. But Preston changed its mind. Deep down in fissures of Preston we could see women with cotton-waste in their hair, and men with square tin cans twisting themselves into doors where they were evidently expected, and perhaps a man with a wooden leg selling sand and Bath bricks from a cart – even as we had left it all at Ashton-on-the-Hill. This was our civilization all over again; the rock out of which we also were hewn! And so Preston was too early to expect it, and the sister to whom one turned for encouragement was deep in *Tonby Waiting* and in full possession of herself. But a little beyond Preston – at some given point – it suddenly occurred. We passed over the edge of things. We were on a mere shelf of land with parochial Lancashire snatching her last belongings and hurrying away behind us over the guard's van and the train rushing on towards the hard, clean edge of things; trees and hedges sloping inwards like streaming hair; windmills with wine in their heads; and before us a washed and strangely empty sky. The porter who took our tickets at Poulton was a beautifully weathered man. We crossed a sharp frontier. The place where this occurred was not marked on the map of the Fylde, and I wonder if I could find it now, as I used to find it every year, on the map of life. Perhaps not! I have given great offence to Blackpool and I no longer catch any look in her eyes. I have burst in without knocking and left without saying "Good-bye". I have been guilty of the grave offence of "running over" and even of going on business, a thing no man should ever do. Several times I have been for the day. I have been there and back in an afternoon, and found our business men as I left them, still at dominoes. I have hardly, indeed, known that I have been, and no one has told it to another of me that I had been to Blackpool. No cab; no agony of doubt as to whether the cab would come in time; no view through cab windows of the fading panorama of Ashton-on-the-Hill, with old men floating in it to whom the incredible fate had happened that they were not going; no home-made bread in the lid of a trunk, "so that we might have a loaf of our own to begin with"; no sense of assurance that someone had all the tickets in his waistcoat pocket; no parkin - nothing but my own dreary sophisticated self. But the first time I did this monstrous thing it occurred to me that I had suddenly turned on my youth and killed it.

Riders to the sea! And what more can be remembered? There was a display of generalship – not the first that day – by the head of the family on a platform, and the next moment, seated in an open carriage – first mark of a civilization more ostentatious than that of Ashton-on-the-Hill – we were driving down a narrow street, devoted to the merchandise of cricket-caps, spades, walking-sticks and "rock", and terminating in the jubilant abyss of low tide. I never knew us to catch the tide "in", but always thus, showing its teeth in the back of its cage. And then a sharp turn to the right; a momentary obscuration of the sea-view; a re-statement of belief in the governing class which rode facing the direction of our progress, that the side streets would be hardly thinkable to stop in, and that Claremont Park was so separated by distance and character as to be hardly Blackpool at all; and the perception by us all that there was a high wind with sand in it. We had arrived. But we had only just arrived. We were in Blackpool, but not yet of it. We were, in fact, *arrivistes*. Blown up a long asphalt walk, deeply compromised with small luggage, and exposed to the disinterested regard of numerous families more settled in than we, our actual arrival constituted a slight social ordeal, and we had the sensation of being only doubtfully within our rights to have come at all. The breeze took the occasion of our entrance to play a rough practical joke on the landlady, who could be seen through frosted glass struggling for a foothold on the oilcloth amid a blizzard of circulars from the Wesleyan Chapel and the Winter Gardens. Having by much combined exertion re-closed the door, and established a reclaimed space in which we could get into *rapport* with the landlady, we were shown up, and in a moment, Providence, with her bonnet strings untied, was laying out her own bread, her own butter, and her own jam on the tablecloth. Far away across the mirror of the wet sands a dog, perceptibly damp even at such a distance, coughed into the face of the sea, and anchored out on the promenade was a carriage, the horse resting on three legs, with one loose one. The pier had the mopes because it was tea-time. Two people came up the asphalt to the next house. They were blown along even as we had been, but had a curious air of being *au fait*, and when someone called to them from an invisible window below, they answered with something gay and reckless and deeply habituated. We were apprised for the first time that a poodle shorn to imitate a lion was staying three doors up, and again we had the feeling that we were looking into an ordered creation out of the chaos of our status. In it but not of it! This thing was going to take some getting into, and it was with a slight sense of discouragement that we turned from the window and took our first look at "The Woman of Samaria" in an oleograph. The cupboard in the chiffonier emitted a powerful odour of Madeira cake, and from the floor below there ascended a tinkling of crockery coupled with the exudations of something frying which was not for us. Strange that a fortnight hence, to leave the habit of that room and the view from that window should come with such an air of annihilation.

For the day and the hour indeed came when we again appeared before Imperial Terrace, this time to undergo sentence of obliteration. It was terrible to stand before Imperial Terrace in one's right mind and one's overcoat, while our larger luggage came out clasped against the diaphragm of the driver and the landlady came with us to the carriage door – light ripples of our sinking. I have seen people watching us with polite concern from garden seats, and their poise, their equilibrium has seemed at the moment that of the everlasting hills. They looked rooted. And we were always cut off in the flower. If we often came in at low tide, I have known us to leave it brimming – sea and sky a basin of blue, the piers no bigger than two caterpillars, the sun striking some flaw in the wrought surface of the sea and splitting into brass, the turnstiles at the end of the pier clocking delicately. I have gone away to the sound of dinner-gongs, and have seen the guests on the steps of boarding-houses stepping down one by one from these high altitudes of conversation to which the sound of dinner-gongs only just carries. And on the way back there was no sharp frontier, but only a fading. Bolton and Moses Gate and Pendleton did not proclaim themselves, but merely occurred as the body went on in a chocolate-coloured carriage and the soul stayed behind. Yet the last stage of our journey was not without a recovering sharpness. Ashton-on-the-Hill reconstructed itself through the cab windows. The old men whose lives had not been enlarged like ours still supported the Town Hall, and we perceived that on the market ground there was a slight eruption of shows. An intensely familiar face cut across the windows like the flight of a white bird. In the house there was a slight flavour of damp, and the back-door key turned with a loud cry of pain, but beyond the back door was the meek, expectant garden, and the butcher's pony which grazed in the field had just reached the far corner of its pasturage and had turned to eat its way back. And the tram-car with its three horses was sprawling up the road to Mossbridge because it was twenty past the hour and that was its appointed time. *Banal!* Oh, how *banal!* And yet – eternal life.

XVII
LET US NOW PRAISE FAMOUS MEN!

WE were acutely aware of London. The first visit to London was a thing which occurred to all of us. It came in due course, like long trousers, because the time seemed ripe for it, and it was doing the youth an injustice to postpone it any longer. Before my own time came, I often heard London discussed among my elders with considerable knowledge of the subject, and my father was fond of testing the reality and accuracy of this knowledge by propounding problems of transit. "How would you get", he would ask, "from Russell Square" (where our boarding-house was) "to Westminster Abbey", or "Can you remember the way from the Nelson column to Hyde Park Corner?" In the arguments which followed, some of the disputants – as they had it this way and that – got rather hopelessly lost, but it was evident that visible if faulty impressions of real streets were agitating their minds. My father was well qualified to act as moderator in these discussions, having at once a greater familiarity with London than any of us, and an inexhaustible interest in the topic. His knowledge of London was extensive but it was not in any way peculiar. It may be said that he knew all the things that were worth knowing in London, but none of the things that weren't. He went so far as to be able to take one to the Albany where Macaulay had lived. He was familiar not only with all the tombs in Westminster Abbey but carried in his mind the names of those who lie beneath flagstones in the Cloisters, and he had one advantage over even the resident population of London in that he had visited the Tower. On the other hand, he knew nothing of resorts – had never heard, for example, of Romano's. About hotels he had no opinion except the opinion that Morley's in Trafalgar Square was a fine palatial place and no doubt very luxurious inside, and his knowledge of restaurants did not go beyond the A.B.C. shops, which he admired exceedingly because the tariff was moderate and it was possible to "pop into one" almost anywhere. Very often in those aforementioned disputes, I have heard him strive to re-establish the exact position of Burlington House or the British Museum by recalling the circumstance that there was an A.B.C. shop almost directly opposite to it. Did the obstinate one not remember being taken in there for something to eat? If I could see my father back again on earth – which I can't – I would meet him more considerately on many points, but the new birth in me which he would the most appreciate, would show itself in this. I would let him off those annual holidays at Blackpool in which, with carefully concealed patience, he trudged backwards and forwards on the asphalt, and forwards and backwards on the boards of the pier with nothing to look at but a sea on which there were no ships, and nothing to do except absorb oxygen, for which in itself he had no passion, while his elder children flirted and the younger dug. I would even let him off Port Erin because I fancy that Port Erin – where we began to go later, also palled on him after a time. And I would of my own initiative suggest that we should go to London in August and prove by experience and keep on proving for fourteen days, his favourite theory that to ride five miles on the top of a London 'bus for threepence was meat and drink at once for the body and mind. I would collect around me in the fag-end of the family – to which I belonged – a party pledged to this noble programme. And I would carry it. Then should I see the love of all history and all the humanities, thoughts of Dr. Johnson, thoughts of Christopher Wren and Charles Lamb, the zest for milky towers against a blue sky with curious crowds of men swarming, kindle new lights in those patient eyes which had seen so little, but had seen so well and seen so deep.

In due time it came to me to be taken to London. I speak of a time which is not after all very long ago, but many things have changed since then and among them, the journey from Lancashire to London. I fear that what has been gained in the journey in time, has been lost in spiritual experience. To-day the best trains pride themselves on swallowing the whole distance at one gulp and the traveller is shot, as though by a catapult, plump into the middle of Euston. Not so when I first went! We approached London gradually. We took nourishment out of paper bags and a collapsible sandwich box and developed the fidgets. We looked out upon Cheshire and upon the Midlands and the Home Counties and finally we looked down into the back gardens between Willesden and Euston and marked the broken perambulators and peeling rocking-horses and the sitz-baths stuck like medals against the back walls of London houses. We stopped for quite a long time at Rugby. It was impossible not to observe the marked differences which distinguished the station at Rugby from our own Victoria in Manchester. Victoria was drab; Rugby was blue like the inside of a shell, and green fields washed up against it like the tides of ocean. There was less ink on fingers and much more soil on shoes. The people who were waiting on the platform wore tweeds, and fox-terriers were attached by steel chains to their experienced luggage. At Rugby the minds of my elders were deeply exercised by thoughts of a certain Arnold who had lived and laboured there. Rugby to them meant "Arnold of Rugby", and I think that my father always intended to break his journey at Rugby in order that he might visit the famous school. I do not know whether this intention was ever carried out, but in the meantime he never failed to gaze earnestly from the carriage window across the fields – in its probable direction.

It was like that all the time we were in London. London meant chiefly the home of the dead – and the living. We were all the time praising famous men. The Temple suggested Dr. Johnson and Charles Lamb. Everywhere we went suggested somebody. We treated London as though it was an extensive cemetery, and it is from this visit and not from any later on – Heaven forgive my degeneration! – that I date my knowledge that Ben Jonson's effigy in the Abbey – I have not since refreshed my recollection but I know it to be true – bears the words "O rare Ben Jonson". I was placed in front of that monument and was bidden to take note of the perfect comprehensiveness and sufficiency of the epitaph. But I said that London meant also the home of the living. And so it did! The climax of the visit occurred when we saw Mr. Gladstone, not in a monument but in his own person, albeit he also had been not a little chiselled and written upon by time and was in fact visibly turning into marble. Seeing Mr. Gladstone was in all respects – except that there was nothing to pay – very like seeing Wembley, calling up all one's faculty of being struck with awe, furnishing in the retrospect almost as much food for thought. It happened this way.

We waited outside the tall gates of Palace Yard. Inside the gates there was little to be seen but there were signs that "the House" was undoubtedly in session. A policeman standing by what was palpably the door, was writing in his note-book, holding it high against the wall. The cab-drivers in the shelter were in a smoky session of their own. Outside the shelter a large congregation of pigeons was collected hopefully around the nose-bags. Someone whom we took to be a Member appeared without his hat at the mouth of a portico, speeded a parting guest and went back into the gloom with long strides, thoughtfully. This was all there was for the moment, but a friendly constable by the gates, pitying our provinciality, had testified of his own knowledge, and for that matter from the witness of his own eyes, that Mr. Gladstone was inside. It was nothing to him, but he surmised that it might be something to us. It was! Moreover, he was able to tell us out of his amazing stores of experience that Mr. Gladstone was almost certain soon to be coming out. Mrs. Gladstone, it appeared, had a few minutes before our arrival driven through in an open carriage to fetch him out. With this guarantee we looked around us – at the omnibuses ploughing the devious channel between flower-beds into Victoria Street, at the tail-coated men carrying red boxes which we knew contained affairs of state, at the towers of the Abbey which were the colour of skimmed milk. And presently the policeman waved us close up to his wing and up the yard we saw, drawn by an unremarkable brown horse, the approach of a low victoria. Mr. Gladstone! His hat appeared at least a size too large for him and beneath the wide brim were his eyes, nearly as deep and dark as the caves we had sometimes gone into with candles, near Buxton. We had the sense of having been gathered up into his eyes because the great man knew his greatness and looked at us, knowing quite well what we were after. And then the carriage passed on, and the top of his hat, jolting slightly over the folded cover of the victoria, was the last thing we saw as it was taken into the sluiceway of Whitehall. But it had been an experience, and by and by in the nearest A.B.C. shop we went over the incident again and again, as people do on the other side of a crisis, and I remember that we were all satisfied that we had retained the presence of mind, as Mr. Gladstone passed, to take off our hats. There was not one in the company who, for the greed of his eyes, had to reproach himself with not having taken off his hat.

Things like these were the meat and drink of those times. Solid and unsentimental men of affairs used to receive from their families at Christmas the acceptable gift of a piece of wood, framed in what was undoubtedly bark and credibly guaranteed, albeit somewhat formal and rectangular in shape, to be an authentic chipping of Mr. Gladstone's axe; and quite a number of people will remember an important observance of our annual holidays in North Wales – how, at a given moment shortly after leaving Chester, and not without some anxiety lest we should miss the chance, we all – family and casual strangers – gazed through the window at what was undoubtedly the wrong chimney-stack, and how it was pronounced by our experienced and travelled elders – the wish that it should be so being father of an obstinate and tenacious opinion that it was – to be "Hawarden, where Mr. Gladstone lives". The edification that proceeded from the house was extremely powerful, and had such a catholicity of truth that it was applicable to life at every point – to mind, morals and mastication. Many mothers of sons knew Mr. Gladstone's habits almost indelicately, and I remember one prophetess in particular, whose Sunday afternoon reading, divided between the doings of the God of Israel in the Scriptures and those of Mr. Gladstone – were they not chronicled in the apocrypha of the Congregationalist press, rarely failed at tea-time to yield some addition to our Gladstoniana – how he bit everything thirty-three times (everybody had that); how he and Mrs. Gladstone once kept their tea hot in a foot-warmer (a real collector's treasure); how he was seen in Hawarden Park throwing a stick for a fox-terrier and how the fox-terrier always brought it back so that he couldn't for the life of him get on with his book, and at last by throwing it further and further

so tired himself out, that the dog wasn't allowed out with him any more; and
how, half an hour before he rose to introduce the Home Rule Bill, he found time
to drop a note to Sir Henry Irving reserving seats at the Lyceum, a slightly
dubious and incomprehensible proceeding, to be set alongside that other
baffling and mysterious fact that he went to church and not, like us, to chapel,
but illustrating in a striking manner the valuable maxim that there is a time for
everything if only one does one thing at a time.

*   *   *

England was soaked in personality about this time – almost as she is soaked
to-day in petrol. Nothing was stirring in the country except the human spirit.
Mechanics was quiet. Science had indeed been very busy, but science was only
a kind of inverted theology. It might – it often did turn the believer into an
agnostic. But it had not yet gone into the entertainment line and had yet to
produce the motor-car, the moving picture, the gramophone, the aeroplane and
the wireless installation. The present universal regard and respect for gadgets
began with the appearance of the bicycle about 1896. All these things were
wanting to the 'eighties and the early 'nineties. On the other hand, what a piece
of work was man! – "how noble in reason! how infinite in faculty! in form and
moving how express and admirable! in action how like an angel! in apprehension
how like a god!" About this time, living in England were Gladstone, Tennyson,
Bright, Browning, Huxley, Irving, W. G. Grace, Gilbert, Sullivan, Darwin,
Newman, Manning, Spurgeon, Liddon, Dale, and lest it should be thought we
are running short, let us throw in further such filberts as Herbert Spencer,
Ruskin, Disraeli, and Carlyle. I think that all these men were alive in 1880. Many
of them were still living in 1890, though a few of them had fallen on sleep. There
was also a very creditable second eleven. The Marquess of Salisbury was of a
somewhat rock-like formation. It used to be said, again, that no country in the
world except England could exhibit such a human phenomenon, composed of
slow speech, perfect disinterestedness, crushing common sense and power to
move large masses of instructed and formidable citizenship this way and that, as
the Duke of Devonshire – the one with the long beard. In 1886, Joseph
Chamberlain had taken such a hold of the imagination of middle-class
Nonconformity that when, in that year, he quarrelled with Mr. Gladstone, it was
in many houses as though there had been a divorce between the two heads of
the family and it was fortunate that it was possible to put Morley on the vacant
pedestal, because in those days the country was furnished with pedestals and on
each pedestal there had to be a man.

And this being our rich condition as to men, there was much more admiration abroad in the country than there is to-day. That age was in fact as much addicted to admiration as the present one is to envy. Much of the time of the ordinary man was spent in being a contemporary; in marvelling at other people's speeches in the House, their sermons at the Tabernacle or St. Paul's, their "Hamlets" at the Lyceum, their "two hundreds" (not out) at the Oval and Old Trafford, and finally, when all else was failing, at the number of years they had been living and still lived. The evaporation of all this authority has been complete, and at this moment I do not know one name current among us – against all those many named just now – which could be depended on to lower all the eyelids in any company wherein it was named. Yes! I know one! But it's not the name of a man. It's Rolls Royce!

XVIII
A CONCLUDING NOTE ON LANCASHIRE

LANCASHIRE calls itself, and is called by others, a county, but it has always given itself the airs of a continent. It has developed within itself frontiers of the highest precision and formality. Everybody who travels between Manchester and Liverpool must have noticed the peculiar vacancy of the view from the carriage window as the train travels across fields which seem to have no purpose except to hold the earth together and grow celery. If our traveller be himself from Manchester he will find himself, before he reaches Liverpool, passing through stations of which he never heard the names, and he will reflect with astonishment that these places are the homes of Lancashire people who have lived there all their lives. It is a frontier between the two cities of Manchester and Liverpool, two cities which are not and never have been really on speaking terms – on writing and telephoning terms but not on speaking terms! If anyone thinks I exaggerate the strangeness of Manchester and Liverpool to one another he may be referred to "Bradshaw", from which he will find that the last tolerable train between the two places is at 9.30 at night, an arrangement which would almost completely prevent social intermixture even if it were desired. It is a curious fact that Liverpool took no part in the Liberal movement of the nineteenth century, the leadership of which was shared between Manchester and Birmingham.

If we extend our survey we shall find still wider variations, still in the same county. One of the boundaries of Lancashire on the north is the River Duddon, which runs in a veritable viaduct of sonnets by Wordsworth, while its south-eastern boundary is the River Tame, the waters of which are black with a blackness which does not come of depth, and very likely, if anyone were bold enough to lap them, are warm. At any rate, I seem to remember having seen a wisp of steam over its course, and, though the Tame is still a melodious stream and goes over a shallow fall between Ashton-under-Lyne and Dukinfield which fills the night-hours with a loud music, its song has come to sound as though it were all about cops and twists and counts and effluents; I can imagine it laughing merrily because somewhere up its course it left a limited company "stopped for bobbins".

And, again, it would be possible to cause the reader, by merely reciting a list of place-names, such a violent change of idea and association as would be quite impossible in Somerset or Westmorland or even in Yorkshire. Thus there is the North Shore at Blackpool. There used to be a peremptory frontier at Blackpool

70

between North and South, those who promenaded and conversed and flirted to the music of a band keeping to the North and regarding the South, where in the open air they danced to music in couples, as slightly infected – but in our own times distinctions like this have been obliterated. Next to Blackpool we might place the Jesuit country round Stonyhurst, and next to Stonyhurst, Strangeways, where Saturday is quite universally the first day in the week and a somewhat historic Nonconformist chapel was recently converted into a synagogue, the tapering portion of the spire being removed to signalize the change from the New Testament to the Old. And almost next door to Strangeways there is Kersal, where conversation is largely carried on in modern Greek and where Vénisélos might easily be staying for the week-end without any of the rest of us being any the wiser; and from Kersal, with its Egyptian cigarettes and its Balkan politics, we might jump to Fleetwood, where I believe they go fishing in the direction of Iceland. But it would still be Lancashire, and, when we had brought all these places within our ambit, and had included, further, Union Street, Oldham, and the shores of Lake Windermere, we should find that we had still forgotten much matter of further diversity – Southport, for example, where good Lancashire people go before they die.

[Conclusion of the original volume]

XIX
AN INTELLECTUAL

He was one of those irritating men who were doubtful about Mr Gladstone. It was an idiosyncrasy. It made him of itself definitely a character, and it is the thing I remember about him principally, and how it constituted him a sort of knot in the grain of our timber. He was doubtful about Mr Gladstone chiefly in an armchair, or if not in an armchair, at home in a first-class carriage of the 10.53 which brought him and the final essence of our citizenship into Manchester every Tuesday and Friday. I have never known in a body of things outwardly very much resembling one another, so similar in the husk, such differences of fruit and kernel, such varieties of content, character, and aroma as were to be found in the trains by which every morning Ashton-on-the-Hill was made tributary to Manchester. When I come to think of them, they were as full of shape and purpose and assumed the consistency of a sonata, which climbs up towards a central movement of import and significance and, having reached and stated it, proceeds with the same deliberation to fall away. And this central movement, approached from a great distance by the hollow and sepulchral theme of the workmen's trains, gathering intelligibility but still lacking warmth and colour in the 8.24 which was a powerful suction of those who got their livings with their coats on, and itself followed by soft pedal passages of the casual travelling of ladies, lawyers' articled clerks, and the clergy, was undoubtedly the 10.53. Few went by it except reputed millionaires, directors of the District Bank, and those who stood with varying success, as Liberal candidates for Hyde and the High Peak. I have seen the stationmaster show them in and wave them off with deference. Mr Darlington, not without a suspicion of cotton waste on his sleeve – for it was a proud feature of our aristocracy that it did not look it – was always of the company, and it was on the 10.53 on Tuesday and Friday morning, as well as in the dining-room of his house which lay somewhat bleak and black but definitely baronial in our hinterland, that he was so doubtful about Mr Gladstone. So, at least, we who were not present understood by filtration.

The smallness of the part which Mr Darlington played in affairs may be estimated by the circumstance that Ashton-on-the-Hill had hardly ever seen him after dark. At Wycliffe itself, if he were not among the "oncers" – a point on which my memory inexplicably fails me, though somehow I associate him deeply with Sunday morning and sunlight and the activity of sparrows behind the glazed windows on the ledge – but if he was not a "oncer" it is certain that Wycliffe was only his spiritual home and that its corridors and vestries and classrooms and all the draped and jewelled precincts which had grown up around it did not serve him as they served us for betrothals and breakings-off, for the arts of speech and music, for statesmanship and career, for the slow but sure disenfoldment of character and all the human comedy, for the meat and drink of social life. I think it can seldom or never have been half-past seven to him. His appearance even at a meeting of the Literary Society was unusual, and always betokened a somewhat exceptional lecture on the Alps or the Tyrol, and since it was generally known among us that, wherever it was, he had been, his presence on the front row acted with all of us who were behind, as a sort of certificate to the authenticity of the more stupendous lantern view. All the same, though his name was on hardly any committee, and he was seldom if ever summoned by Mr Ogden Green's postcards to meetings of an "executive", nor was yet one of the team which could be put with confidence to the wicket of public prayer, it was always understood that it was not because he was beneath but, if anything, rather above such honours. To me he will always be a memorable and somewhat awful figure as the first and almost the only real Liberal Unionist I ever saw in private life. In this respect of Liberal Unionism he was as solitary as Satan. He assumed the high scientific interest of the abstruse specimen – a chunk of lava; an exhibit on our own beach of some cosmic happening in the murmuring sea. Reflection on the subject, started by the scraps of table-talk on which I was nourished and for that matter still live - was stimulated by his high and towering visibility during long periods of time in which the mind craved for food. It was his habit to stand sentry at his pew door during all the petitionary part of our ritual. He was knee-deep even in our second and more prolonged prostration, a monument visible on the most distant coasts of Wycliffe, and casting a deep shadow over the nearer slopes on which I was browsed. Many a time have my own private fidgets been caught and fastened by his blue eye pinned to the back of a varnished pew as a butterfly is pinned on cardboard.

I think that my memories of Mr Darlington must be deeply coloured by his habit of carrying about with him the monthly reviews. On Sunday mornings, at any rate, he was never seen save in the company of Huxley and Tyndall, and his progress from the door of his carriage to the door of his pew was harassed by large and slippery quantities of the best that was at that moment of time being said and thought. Perhaps I build too much on this, but I do not think so. It stamped him. After all, were there not citizens of Ashton-on-the-Hill, also astir and abroad on Sunday mornings, from whose custom of carrying – also under the arm – an assortment of abstruse and valetudinarian dogs we read perspicuous volumes on the theme of character and destiny? And not only did it stamp Mr Darlington but it stamped us. This hawking of the "Nineteenth Century", this distribution over the pew-backs of "Blackwood" and the "Fortnightly", was a thing which simply did not occur among the minor heretics of Ashton-on-the-Hill, nor did I ever hear of its happening at the Parish Church. It was a contact; a slight enlargement of experience, and just as the shutters to Miss Wrigley's bonnet and Mr Surridge's frock-coat of the best broadcloth indicated the still pools of faith and the sufficiency of the soul unto itself, and my own gloves and threepenny-bit, the odour of black silk around me, and the contact of jet trimmings with the cheek in sleep were all profoundly stagnant and levitical, so did Mr Darlington's reviews – the monthlies and the quarterlies – effect some change of key and exhibit us in the aspect also of citizens of the world; Athenians who were not averse either to tell or to hear some new thing: to some extent en rapport; not wholly unacquainted with what Mr Gladstone had done to Professor Huxley about the Scriptures – or was it the other way about? And I think that if I were making a list of those who impinged mightily upon our youth and seem now so strangely dwarfed across the fissure which has occurred in time, I should set down many – Dr E. M. Grace, Murdoch, Spofforth, and the Australians, Mr Schnadhorst, and a whole galaxy of eminent private members, slightly side-whiskered, admirably trousered and shod, carrying dramatically into our public assemblies latest tidings from some interminable battle which was waging with the parson and the squire; and, having marshalled all these, I should of my own contribution add Mr Darlington. He also dabbled in those low, pacific tides of human circumstance. He was the kind of man who very likely predicted this war. I should feel sure that he had predicted it but that every age has its bogy, and in his the bogy was Russia.